Praise for *Moonlight In MudPuddles*

The book depicts vulnerability as a strength...an asset to reach the unreachable. It pushes you to come up with your own truth, rather than fall into a pattern that was only developed in your mind because others told you it was so. The book allows you the permission to heal and reminds you that boundaries are essential. I highly recommend this read to anyone who has a pulse. Growth happens; it's not just a book. —Jen Tveraa, Adult Felony Probation & Parole Officer

Moonlight in Mud Puddles is a captivating and emotional read that celebrates the duality in the journey of life, taking the reader along for the ride. I found myself both laughing and crying when reading this. Dr. Cecil shares intense past experiences, the science of trauma, clinical experience, and humor while finding true self love. Anyone who has ever struggled to understand themselves should read this book. In a beautiful dance between past and present, Dr. Cecil reminds us that we cannot run from ourselves and that we don't need to. —Chelsey Duenow, Licensed Addiction Counselor

Kedric H. Cecil weaves his personal story with psychological theories and affecting insights from tumultuous experiences of his own and others. Speaking both from personal depth and insights into the lives of others, the winding path of this book involves and inspires the reader. He includes conversations between himself as a young man and as a mature doctor of psychology. Hope is the glue which holds this book together, reflected like the image of its evocative title. —Marcia Melton, author

I recently had the pleasure of reading Ric Cecil's book. I enjoyed the read very much and learned a lot more about my friend than I previously knew. It was an enjoyable ride through his life experiences that resulted in his realization of what his clarity of truth is, thus enabling him to reach out to help others heal from the same maladies that occupied much of his youth.

As an author myself, I found Ric's use of his life experiences to reference his problems and solutions to be an effective way to share with others how life 'happens'!

There is no formula that works the same for everyone, and it is the differences that offer up solutions we may not have access to within our individual 'self'. Ric does a great job of sharing with the reader that everyone has something to offer regardless of how we may feel about ourselves at any given time. That is perhaps the hardest thing to get across to any person who is distracted from seeing with clarity. Ric makes this quite clear in his quest. —Jerry McGowan, author

Moonlight in Mud Puddles

The Continuing Transformation of the Street Kid

Kedric H. Cecil, Ph.D.

Raven Publishing
Norris, MT
Giving wings to great books since 2002

Moonlight in Mud Puddles
The Continuing Transformation of the Street Kid

ISBN: 978-1-937849-51-1
Copyright © 2018 by Kedric H. Cecil, Ph.D.
author of *Wisdom From the Streets*
www.wisdomfromthestreets.com
Cover art copyright © 2018 by Sarah Morris
www.thegirlwhopaints.com

Published by Raven Publishing, Inc. P.O. Box 2866, Norris, MT
www.ravenpublishing.net

Library of Congress Cataloging-in-Publication Data

Names: Cecil, Kedric H., author.
Title: Moonlight in mud puddles : the continuing transformation
of the street kid / Kedric H. Cecil, Ph.D.
Description: Norris, MT : Raven Publishing, [2019] | Includes
bibliographical references and index.
Identifiers: LCCN 2019001310 (print) | LCCN 2019009972
(ebook) | ISBN 9781937849528 (ebook) | ISBN 9781937849511
(trade pbk. : alk. paper)
Subjects: LCSH: Cecil, Kedric H. | Psychologists--United
States--Biography. |Street children--United States--Biography.
Classification: LCC BF109.C4 (ebook) | LCC BF109.C4 C43
2019 (print) | DDC 150.92 [B] --dc23
LC record available at https://lccn.loc.gov/2019001310

To my four amazing adult children,
Clint, Eric, Brian, and Amanda.
Each outstanding in your own unique way,
intelligent and independent, creative and confident,
loving and living life to the fullest.
You have always been my inspiration and motivation
to get back on track, and it is such a privilege
to be part of your "Wisdom Journey."

Acknowledgments

There are always many people who provide the inspiration and motivation for a book of this nature. Many of them are included by name directly or by reference to an experience we shared: friends, family, former students, and patients. I could never produce a complete list, but please know I celebrate every moment of our time together. Thank you for your contribution to this writing.

I want to directly acknowledge and thank Mandy Giesick, whose computer, clerical, and literary skills helped bring the book to completion. Mandy offered invaluable perspective and insight from her own life's struggles, on her journey to personal empowerment and becoming a Reiki Practitioner. Mandy M. Giesick
ammacgies80@gmail.com

The amazing cover art is an original painting by exceptional artist and good friend, Sarah Morris, whose unique style shows the vibrancy and excitement of living life to the fullest. Sarah says, "My paintings are attempts to reach toward the eternal through the vivid lens of my own life's moments." Thank you Sarah, for accepting the task of illustrating the title, and doing it so magnificently.
Sarah Morris Fine Art
thegirlwhopaints.com

TABLE OF CONTENTS

The Conversation
(inside my head)

Street Kid

In *Wisdom from the Streets*, you wrote about gaining Wisdom from Failure. Are you the Wisdom...and I'm the Failure?

Therapist

Are you kidding? Without you...I would have been stuck in an existence of mediocrity without direction or purpose. You are certainly not the failure, you are the Teacher!

Street Kid

What? I never even wanted to be a Street Kid, let alone some kind of Teacher. I have issues!

Therapist

But don't you understand? Without the issues, I would not have been able to see the need to get better, and I would have learned nothing. Those are the exact qualifications which make you the Teacher.

Moonlight in Mud Puddles

Street Kid

Wow! So in this book, will I still be called the Street Kid? How about just calling me Doc?

Therapist

Okay Doc. Maybe I'll just refer to myself as Kedric when we talk… you know, that's actually my real first name, anyway.

———◈◈◈◈———

Doc

For my first Lesson, I want you to come outside in the rain.

Look at the way the moonlight reflects in the water of the mud puddle breaking into so many colors. We all love to see the Moonlight on the surface of a beautiful lake, but it's even more spectacular when you see it on the muddy water.

Kedric

Wow that's cool… but what's the Lesson?

Doc

In my life, I've had a lot of times when I felt buried in the proverbial mud up to my ears, without even a hint of light to show me the way out. But, when I see the moon-light shine in a mud puddle, I'm reminded that the *light* needs the *dark* to show it's beauty, and I know there's a bright side to every situation if I look hard enough.

Kedric

Kind of like feeling that you just need to start being inspired again, and do whatever it takes to get back on track?

Doc

Exactly. I think of Van Morrison singing, "Come and go with me to the Bright Side of the Road."

Kedric

Oh, I love that song!

Doc

Somehow when I hear it, I begin to believe I will find the light again if I do what it takes to dig my heart out of the mud, because a whole new world of opportunity is waiting right across the road. *Moonlight in Mud Puddles* speaks to the amazing synchronicity that happens when the *dark* and the *light* impact each other to bring balance and harmony into all the world. Instead of running back and forth between the extremes, we need to embrace the function of both, and be inspired when the Moonlight is reflected in the places we feel stuck the most.

Kedric

But sometimes it feels so Dark, for so long.

Doc

Of course. Just remember, someday all your mud puddles will produce the most amazing life lessons to brighten

Moonlight in Mud Puddles

everything around you. Sometimes, when you feel stuck in it up to your ears, (no matter what "it" actually is) the moonlight will be the only thing that reflects enough inspiration to pull you through to the other side.

Kedric

Awesome! I said you were the Teacher.

Doc

Now, let me tell you about the first time I realized how magical the image of the moonlight can be when I feel like I have nothing left to live for.

You remember, it happened one time when I was on the run, and...

1

The Sadness Shield

Douglas: Will you keep out all the sadness?
Max: I have a sadness shield that keeps all the sadness out
and it's big enough for all of us.
Maurice Sendak
Where the Wild Things Are (the movie)

I love the waterfront. I love the sounds from the old
wooden planks of the docks that move and creak in response to the caresses of the water below. I love the smell
of fish in the air that hangs like a strong perfume, which
assaults and excites the senses at the same time, beckon-
ing me to seek out a place of peace and safety.

On the waterfront, sometimes the wind brings a pen-
etrating cold that chills every fiber of my being, yet for a
thirteen-year-old runaway, it is one of the warmest and
safest places I can hang out during the day.

I love the waterfront because, with all the excitement
and activity, nobody pays any attention to me. People
pass me on the sidewalks and some even nod in acknowl-
edgment, assuming we are mutual participants in seeking out the interesting and exotic attractions offered by

the places in downtown Seattle on Elliott Bay.

But I am not a tourist. I am on the waterfront because I am engaged in the greatest of all human struggles—I am alone on the streets—and I must survive.

<hr />

Survival means different things to people depending on their situation. To me, it meant not having to go home. The strangest thing is that I didn't know why I had to run away. I just *had* to.

Many people on the streets, both adults and kids don't have a home to go back to—but I did. I lived in a nice house one block up from Lake Washington with a nice view and nice people, including my mom, little sister, grandma, my step-father, and his two daughters who lived with us in the summer.

Life should have been really good for me as a seventh-grader in a nice school, with a nice family, in a nice city, but...for some unknown reason, as a twelve- to thirteen-year-old boy, I preferred being home-*less* to being home-*more*.

But why can't I remember anything about life at the house or even why I wanted to run away?

Often, when I try to think of things that happened at the lake house, I see a flashback of a room someplace else.

Most cities had an abundance of flophouse hotels, with cheap rooms that I could sometimes afford if I had hustled enough that day. In my mind's eye, the image is fleeting, but I remember the *hotel room.*

6

The Sadness Shield

I cannot see the lobby of the hotel, or even the stairs or hall-way leading to the farthest room down to the end on the left, overlooking the street. But as I open the door, I see the same scene every time.

The pale blank walls, which may have once been white, are stained yellow by years of tobacco smoke, illuminated in shadows by a single light bulb which hangs down on a long, twisted cord from a high ceiling in the middle of the room. A small, worn-out bed with a wrought-iron frame is pushed tight-ly against one wall, with a beat-up three-drawer dresser with most of the handles missing, on the opposite side of the room.

The dresser has long curved sides on top to hold a mirror, which has long since been broken and removed.

There's a small, colorless, oval throw rug on a cold linoleum floor by the side of the bed, and a wooden chair next to the window overlooking the reddish hotel sign that blinks on and off throughout the night, bleeding through flimsy curtains to cast an eerie, pulsating light on the garish yellow walls.

When I see that image in my mind, I always enter the room and sit down on the chair overlooking the street and stare blank-ly out the window.

I am alone, but not afraid.

I'm just glad I'm not on the streets tonight or at the house overlooking the lake.

I recently asked my younger sister, Libby, what she re-membered about the time in Seattle, when we lived at the lake house because I remember so little. She reminded me that being five years younger than me, she was six or seven years old and in the first grade.

"I don't have a lot of memories at the Lake City house," she said. "I remember the layout of the house and the yard, which had a fence around the front. I remember that fence because Wayne, our new stepfather, put nails sticking out of the top to rip up neighborhood dogs that were jumping into our yard. I remember that he was mean to animals and years later, Mother told me he was mean to you, too.

"I also have a few, very limited memories of his relationship with Mother. I have a brief memory of her jumping out of the passenger door of the car in the middle of traffic. They must have been fighting as he drove the car. I remember looking out of the window and seeing her on her hands and knees on the side of the road, in tears and struggling to get up. I also remember being horrified."

"Wow," I said, as she told me these things. "I've never even heard that they had a troubled marriage. I have always felt that the only trouble in that house was ME."

Libby replied, "I know you don't remember Grandma Bea living in the basement, and I'm not sure if you were even there the time that I was standing at the top of the stairs just off the kitchen where Wayne and Mother were fighting loudly. Grandma Bea came to the bottom of the stairs and, looking past me, called up to ask if everything was all right. I remember Mother was crying, and it seems to me that Wayne had some chains in his hands. When Grandma Bea intervened, he walked away.

"I also have a vague recollection of being in the back

seat of the car at night, when we were driving around downtown Seattle, looking for you. I remember that Wayne was driving, and when we couldn't find you, it made him mad."

At this point, my sister looked up and said, "Don't you remember any of this? It's hard to believe that you don't remember the rowboat trip across the lake, even after hearing about it from Marcy."

I had just returned from reconnecting with my stepsister in Portland, Oregon, who I had not seen since those troubled times long ago. Marcy recounted a memory of her father being mad at me because I was playing with a ball in the backyard and had stepped on some of his shrub bushes. When I told her I couldn't even remember the backyard, she exclaimed, "Well at least you remember the trip across the lake in the rented rowboat. Karen said she was terrified."

Marcy related that in preparation for our meeting, she had been talking to her little sister, Karen, who was about Libby's age. Karen related to her that she remembered being in a rowboat with me in the middle of Lake Washington, scared to death as she watched huge seaplanes landing on the water.

I replied to her, "I have mostly blank spots about that time period, but it's hard to imagine not remembering being in a rowboat in the middle of a huge lake with one of my stepsisters who I can barely remember at all."

I told Libby about Karen's recollections, after returning from my visit with Marcy in Portland. Libby responded, "That was me in the boat, and I remember it well!

Moonlight in Mud Puddles

"I know we were staying at a cabin on the other side of the lake because Mother was taking some classes. You were supposed to be taking care of me—you were always a terrible babysitter.—We rented a boat and you took off across the lake. I don't remember Karen being with us, but she may have been—maybe we picked her up when we got to the other side.

"Anyway, I remember the trip back. I was worried that we were going to get in trouble because I knew we were doing something wrong. You were too exhausted to row, and I got out of the boat and tried to push it from behind because I knew we had to get back. I remember looking over the back of the boat when I was in the water, kicking with little effect to push us forward. Anyway, after we pulled up on shore, Mother and the man who rented the boat were there. I know he was angry and disgusted. I think Mother was relieved, thinking we might all have drowned. As I said, you were a terrible babysitter."

I, of course, thanked Libby for the memories—Marcy and Karen, too.

But I find myself thinking, *I am not troubled by the things I remember. I am troubled by the things I don't.*

A lot of people ask me how I became a runaway and what I did with my time on the streets. The answer is simple:

I often don't know.

The memories come in pieces but are often hidden in places where the doors are locked. Without even being aware of blocking out something, I learned to flip a switch in my mind and retreat into my imagination, as I had done since childhood. I had music, conversation, and an amazing variety of interactive entertainment.

And there, the monsters were not allowed.

I have a lot of lost time. Time that I miss with all my heart—and time that I hope stays lost forever.

<hr />

The times as a runaway that I do remember offer enough lessons for my "Wisdom Journey" to last a lifetime.

Like the time I met Judy.

I met her walking up the hill from First Avenue. She was cute and smiled at me as I walked next to her. She said she was walking up to Fifth Avenue to catch a bus to the University District where one of her girlfriends was having a party.

I remember thinking, *Awesome! This girl is a student at the University of Washington that is going to be my girlfriend. All I have to do is convince her that, instead of being a 13-year old runaway, I'm a 22-year old adult that she should take with her to the party.*

The first idea that popped into my head was to offer her a ride. "I'm not doing anything tonight, so instead of taking the bus, why don't you just ride with me, because I'm going that way anyway?"

She responded, "That sounds great! Maybe you'd like to come to the party?"

Of course, I didn't have a car. So with that old familiar feeling of impending doom, I started looking for a way out, while still hoping to go to the party.

Moonlight in Mud Puddles

When we got to the parking space where the phantom vehicle was supposedly parked, I suddenly exclaimed, "It was right here! It's a candy-apple red 1958 Chevy Impala with white leather interior and chrome lake-pipes up the side. I knew I shouldn't have parked such a cool car on a side street in downtown Seattle!"

Judy proclaimed, "You have to call the police!"

We walked together into a nearby hotel lobby and, with a very concerned Judy listening closely, I called the police, described my car, and gave them my Mother's license plate number—APL100—being the only one I could think of on such short notice.

My concerned, caring companion immediately offered to have me ride the bus to the party, and even offered to pay the fare because I had "left my wallet in the car."

The sad telling of my tale was a big hit at the party, as Judy described the ordeal, although a couple of her close friends seemed to regard me with a lot of suspicion. I spent the rest of the night drinking and telling them that it was "becoming too painful to talk about," so they would leave me alone.

At 5:00 the next morning, all remaining males were told to leave, and after asking Judy for her phone number, I was suddenly back on the street with no money and no place to go.

My mind was screaming; *Why did I give the police my mother's license plate number? If they call her, they will find out who I really am and put out a warrant for my arrest! I've gotta get back downtown so I can hide!*

The Sadness Shield

Hiding is what I do best. But what am I hiding from? Who cares! That's my old life. I need to forget my old life. I've got more important things to think about. I'm going to head down by the Beanery and scam a bowl of soup. Or maybe I'll hit Pike Street and hustle some action. It doesn't get any better than this.

As a runaway, I often thought about trying to go back to places we had lived before where I had friends and life made better sense, and somehow, all the broken pieces would magically come together again. After I started running away from the house on the lake, I found myself, one day hitchhiking over Snoqualmie Pass to Sunnyside, Washington, a couple of hundred miles from Seattle. I say that I found myself on the highway because, like a lot of things, I have no memory of how I traveled the ten miles south through the city to get to the main highway—but I remember the trip.

I got a ride with a young guy with a souped-up car and a Ham radio who identified his call sign as "The Anacortes Hot Rod." He was friendly and showed me how the two-way communication worked and even bought me lunch. He took me all the way to Yakima, leaving me with only 50 miles to my destination.

I was sad to see him go and couldn't tell him that what I really wanted was to go back to Anacortes with him, get a job working on souped-up cars, and become an awesome Ham radio operator myself. So, instead, like many brief, intense relationships along the way, which could have given me a new path to happiness, I simply switched off those desires and told myself I didn't want that, anyway.

I thought to myself, W*hy would I want to live in some obscure place as a mechanic with a Ham radio hobby anyway? Life is too short to get stuck with a dead-end job with no future. I've got places to go and people to see. I can't wait to get to Sunnyside where all my friends are going to celebrate with me when they realize what real freedom is. It doesn't get any better than this!*

When I arrived in Sunnyside on a Thursday, I discovered that a carnival was set up in a park near downtown. Being over 6-feet tall, and already used to presenting myself as an adult who was looking for action, I asked the carnival owners if they had a position worthy of someone with my skills. After reassuring them that I was 16-years old, and had to quit high school in Arkansas after both parents were killed in a car accident, they gave me a job setting up bowling pins that people tried to knock over with a softball to win a prize. They also told me that this was a job that could lead to bigger things in the carnival world. If I did a good job, I could eventually become the main guy in the booth, actually taking the money from people and handing out the prizes. They also described a future with positions like operating the Ferris wheel—or maybe even the Tilt-a-Whirl!

Best of all, they told me that I could sleep behind the booth and also travel with them when the carnival left town.

It had only been a year since I had left Sunnyside in

the sixth grade, and now I was off to see the world as a "carny," with friends and co-workers that I hoped would become my new family.

On Saturday, several of my old friends from Mrs. Haas' sixth-grade class, came by to say hello. I could tell that they were impressed—if not a little confused—by my new role as a carny, but we didn't get much chance to hang out, because I had to work. I told them a modified version of my cover-story in that my mother was killed in a car accident in Seattle, and I was now on my own.

Later that afternoon, one of them brought my old scoutmaster by the booth, who insisted that I come with him to his shoe store because he had, "something he wanted to give me."

My first thought was that he was going to provide work boots for my job, but when he came out of the back room of the store, he handed me the phone and said,

"Somebody wants to talk to you." On the phone, my dad in Ashland, Oregon, said, "Ric, this story about your mother isn't true, is it?" Embarrassed and ashamed, I admitted that I made the whole thing up so I could run away.

———————

Kedric

Did you ever think that if you wanted to be a "Carny," without getting caught, you might go someplace where you wouldn't be recognized?

Moonlight in Mud Puddles

Doc

I didn't go to Sunnyside because I wanted to be a "Carny," I went because I wanted to go where my life would be the same again. The carnival just seemed like a good opportunity.

Kedric:

Yeah…an opportunity for more Chaos!

Doc

Even today, I'd rather be a "Carny" than to go back to the house of horrors.

———

Neither my dad, nor my scoutmaster asked why I wanted to run away from such a nice home, but I probably couldn't have told them anyway. I just knew that I had to get away, but now all that was over, and arrangements were made to get me back to Seattle. Back to the house on the lake at 107XX Lakeside Ave. N. E.!

The exact address is burned into my memory, but why can't I remember the things that happened there?

But I *do* remember. I just thought it was a Dream.

I'm kneeling in the northeast corner of the living room, looking out at Lake Washington. It's a beautiful spring day with the sunlight reflecting on the water like diamonds. That's what I need—a thousand diamonds to take with me. Oh, what places I'd go. Oh, wow, here comes the awesome hydroplane, Miss Hawaii Kai, the winner of the Gold Cup! You can spot

16

her way down the lake with those shiny shades of pink—and look at the rooster tail spraying water hundreds of feet in the air.

All of a sudden I'm in the cockpit. I'll go all the way down to the floating bridge at the south end of the lake and attach wings and fly toward the Hawaiian Islands—or the moon—or anywhere but here.

***Here*?**

*How did I get over **There**?*

As the hidden image begins to appear, I can see myself curled up across the room on the dining room floor. My stepfather is kicking me as I try to cover my head.

There's no pain—no sound—nothing at all.

Wow, that was weird. One minute I'm having a really good day watching Miss Hawaii Kai out on the lake, and the next I'm seeing myself being kicked and beaten.

Funny how the mind plays tricks on you.

In a recent conversation with my 94-year old mother, she very astutely pointed out that while she remembers most of the events in my life as I have written them, she was astonished at the things I have forgotten. She reminded me that her mother lived with us during part of the year after we moved to Seattle.

"You used to spend a lot of time in the basement with her."

One of the most interesting things about my grandmother living with us is that my lack of memory does not diminish her contribution to my life. I am certain that I would have run away more often if not for her nurturing and warmth.

I just don't remember her in the basement apartment because of what was happening upstairs. I don't remember much about ANY events in the house—or life during the time we lived there.

I am sometimes surprised that I remember The Anacortes Hot Rod." We never know when the briefest moments of kindness may make a significant impact on the lives of those who need it most. I also believe that being accepted for those few hours, fueled by my brief fantasy of becoming like him, he has stayed embedded in my subconscious mind until such a time as this. I salute his memory.

———

I never went back to Sunnyside. That's the last place I remember belonging, with all the members of the band together in Mrs. Haas' class. Most of them missed the opportunity to see me as a carny.

I've often wondered if the carnival people noticed that I didn't return, even to get my pay. I wonder if they asked themselves, "Say, whatever happened to that nice young man from Arkansas? You know, the one whose parents had been killed and was forced to make his way so early in life."

Sometimes I imagine going back on Monday as they were packing up to hit the road. They would say to me, "Hey, where you been? We waited an extra hour hoping you'd come back."

I certainly blew my chance, because, by this time, I

could have been one of the best Ferris Wheel operators that the world has ever known.

And who knows—maybe even the Tilt-a-Whirl.

2
In a Trance

"There were people who had trances, I had surely heard of
them, and they followed strange laws of which we could
know nothing, they obeyed the tangled orders
of their own subconscious minds."
Daphne du Maurier
Rebecca

As stated in *Psychological Trauma and the Developing Brain,*
"Dissociation is a defensive strategy that traumatized
children use to cope with overwhelming feelings. They
often find themselves entering a trance state, where
they do not think, feel or remember."
A woman walked into my office for her second appointment carrying an unusually large cloth handbag that appeared handcrafted. She sat down on the floor a few feet in front of me and said, "Our first session impressed me so much that I think you might be the one man I can trust enough to share this experience with...."

Then she pulled out a loaded Smith & Wesson .357 magnum with a 6-inch barrel and said, "I want to kill myself, but I'm afraid to do it alone. I want you to be here with me while I complete my heart's greatest desire."

Moonlight in Mud Puddles

As I looked into her eyes, I could see that she was serious—perhaps more serious than anything in her life.

I instantly related because of times in the past when I felt that I had nothing left to live for. She was right about choosing me as someone who would understand.

In the intensity of that moment between us, with our eyes locked together in mutual awareness, I suddenly felt a rush of emotion and quietly started to cry. I said to her, "I can really feel your pain."

The next few moments brought such a feeling of to-getherness as we both shared the hurt of long-repressed memories that seem too much to deal with anymore. We also shared the unspoken truth that what happens next will define both of us for the duration of our lives.

There was nothing in my training that covered what to do in such a dilemma.

If she kills herself in my office, that is likely to put a major dent in my private counseling practice.

If I grab the gun and restrain her till the police arrive, that is likely to put a major dent in her trust of me, and she is still going to use the gun when she gets the chance.

My life and my experiences are called to this moment. Nothing outside of it exists.

I asked to handle the gun.

She replied, "No, because you won't give it back."

I said, "Yes, I will."

She stated, "It would be against the law for a licensed therapist to give a loaded gun to a suicidal patient."

I flatly explained, "I don't give a rip about that. This is between you and me, and my word is my bond."

She cautiously handed the gun to me with a look that seemed to say, "I have been lied to many times."

I took the gun, emptied the cylinder, twirled the gun around a little, put the bullets in one-by-one, shut the cylinder and handed it back to her loaded.

Then I said, "You are right. I do understand the need to stop the pain, and if you choose to end your life today, I will be here, so you are not alone. But, since you were right about being able to trust me, is it possible that you would work with me in therapy one week at a time to see if we can ease your pain?

"You can always bring the gun."

Fortunately for both of us, we worked together in therapy sessions for over two years as we plumbed the depths of *Dissociative Identity Disorder* formerly known as *Multiple Personality Disorder.* She brought her bag to every session, but I never saw the gun again.

The reason she felt enough trust to share this experience came in her first session the previous week.

As she sat comfortably on the couch responding to my probing questions about her reasons for seeking therapy, I happened to ask if she sometimes felt like there were other parts of herself in control.

Her response was to lean her head to the left side and fall asleep as if in a trance.

I waited for a few minutes and softly said her name. She was confused for a moment and then said, "What was the question?"

This unusual response suggested probing childhood memories. Since I suspected an abuse history, I shared some of my background. She seemed to brighten and became more responsive as I went on to describe goals to pursue in future sessions.

I felt good about the session and was looking forward to our next time together.

————❦————

Dissociation is the name for the process of blocking from conscious awareness experiences that are unwanted or unnecessary. We all dissociate every day to some extent by becoming distracted, daydreaming, etc.

An example of this is driving the same road every day and not remembering if you passed a particular checkpoint. Recall comes, but usually only with an effort to look around at familiar sites before realization.

The memories of the abused child are often buried much deeper and dissociation is the process by which the trauma can be moved deep within the subconscious to a storage facility where the doors are locked.

Noted Psychiatrist, Bessel van der Kolk states in his book *The Body Keeps the Score: Brain, Mind, and Body in Healing of Trauma*

> *"Traumatized people chronically feel unsafe inside their bodies: the past is alive in the form of growing interior discomfort. Their bodies are constantly bombarded by visceral warning signs, and, in an attempt to control these processes, they often become expert at ignoring their gut feelings, and in numbing awareness of what is played out inside. They learn to hide from themselves."*

24

When an unforeseen incident triggers an implicit memory of "forgotten" abuse, the adult responds like the traumatized child.

As an adult, I am often bewildered by an almost overwhelming feeling that I want to run away from any present experience that seems precarious.

Trauma impacts our lives in a variety of ways, but for a child or adolescent who suffers abuse at the hands of a parent or caretaker, dissociation provides them a way to stay connected to the parent, whom they rely upon for food and shelter, without having to cope with abuse from a caretaker. Complex trauma is the term used to describe abuse which is repetitive and takes place over a period of time, rather than a single event or experience of a traumatic nature. Any traumatic experience may have a devastating impact on the psychophysiology of the brain, but repeated abuse impacts the developing brain associated with specific neurological impairment.

Damage to self-concept and identity; problems regulating emotion, and alterations in consciousness and memory, are but a few effects in which the brain becomes dysfunctional when responding to an abusive environment.

As stated in *Wisdom from the Streets,*

> *"I don't know how many times I actually ran away, how often I was without a safe place to sleep, why I was even there at all—it all just seems jumbled up in my mind and stuck there in my thirteen-year-old self."*

Most people have different facets of their personality developed in part from experiences in their childhood and adolescence. The person who suffers from Dissociative Identity Disorder, however, is often unaware of the other parts because each one has a specific job in protecting the person without being needed all the time. Rather than being an integrated whole person, they live without "co-consciousness" in fragmented lives in which one alter may have no memory of time or actions experienced by one of the others.

Another patient with *Dissociative Identity Disorder* that I was treating at the same time as the .357 lady (as I refer to her) called my secretary one day to cancel her appointment and then showed up 15 minutes early with no recollection of canceling.

After working with both patients individually for several months, I was able to bring them together to give each someone to relate their feelings. They both felt they were "like sisters."

Both patients were victims of repeated physical and sexual abuse as children, and being unable to cope with it in their vulnerable minds, split off into fantasy parts of themselves designed subconsciously to help get through the task of survival.

As the .357 lady worked with me in therapy, she identified at least nine separate alternate personalities or "alters," which were developed as a preschool child who was being horrifically abused. Each one was identified by name according to their role or some association with their function. One was called, "He" and was tough and masculine and ready to lash out, verbally or physically, when she felt threatened. Another named "Susan" was soft and sensuous when marital intimacy was needed.

On one occasion, "Susan" provocatively invited her husband to the bedroom after he cleaned up, and then she fell asleep. When her husband woke her, it was "He" who was present, and, without any awareness of the invitation, a major fight ensued.

There were also two small children within, one who could write and one who could color, as their only means of communication. She later shared that the contents of the cloth bag contained items for each alter, including letters and artwork assigned in session, color crayons and coloring books, etc.

Some of her writing included "mirror writing" in which she could write with the letters reversed, requiring a mirror to read.

"Will Robbins" was an alter whose job was to "run away fast" when anyone got too close.

As this name was discussed, we discovered that as a preschooler, she had watched a television series called *Space Family Robinson* and the family robot kept urging the boy to run from danger by saying, "Run away, Will Robinson...run away fast!" In her child's mind, she heard "Will Robbins," and he took her away from the unbearable reality she could not face on her own.

Toward the completion of her therapy process, my patient wrote a beautiful letter addressed to her different alters.

She named each one, thanking them for the specific role that each played in keeping her safe in past trauma.

Moonlight in Mud Puddles

She then encouraged each to work together as one, because, "It just gets too crazy going off in different directions."

———————

Treatment for a person with *Dissociative Identity Disorder*, or any victim of a traumatic experience, is a complex process beyond the scope of this writing. Therapy involves a cognitive restructuring in which the patient confronts past experiences in an atmosphere of trust and caring and learns to cope with them in a new way by forming a different, more self-empowering feeling about the impact of the experience upon their life.

As they become more able to consciously take control of their increasingly healthy thought processes, they are able to embrace the past as lessons needed to empower, not fragment, their emerging sense of self.

Without realizing it at the time I, too, often ran away from conflict, or from angry companions, by checking out psychologically at least, and physically if possible.

Even though I was aware of my actions, I would often subconsciously "run back into the corner" by filling my life with any escape behavior that took away the image of the trauma across the room.

———————

Kedric

What do you mean, "run back into the corner?" Why would you imagine being in that house for any reason?

Doc

It's not that I want to be anywhere near that house. But when I'm self-destructive, it seems like making it all happen again, and the corner is my escape.

Kedric

Instead of running anywhere, maybe not being so self-destructive would be a better option.

Doc

How about a little credit for time served? I'm getting there!

———❧❧❧———

It has been shown as related in *Psychological Trauma and the Developing Brain* that

> *"abuse and neglect typically sever children not only from their feelings but also from their bodies. Unsafe environments have taught them to ignore all sensory input—to become invulnerable to pain."*

But it feels like it is more than physical and psychological "numbing."

It sounds crazy but...

*Most of the time when I visualize watching myself in the corner, it feels like I am **actually there**.* I offer no rational explanation for this as a possibility, but the corner was my reality, not the event taking place across the room.

In my own healing process, I have become able to reframe my dissociative experience as the greatest training I could ever imagine to help others with similar prob-

Moonlight in Mud Puddles

lems. I am often astounded by the stories of other abuse victims with similar experiences, and how not only time seems to be suspended, but also the laws of physics as we know them.

Since it is my conscious mind by which I know myself, it's amazing to think, *I have a brain that is capable of protecting me when I'm not able to protect myself.*

I don't understand how that could be even close to reality, but my answer for such a possibility is a quote from *Hamlet: There are more things in heaven and earth than are dreamt of in your philosophy.*

I stand in awe of the process.

3
A Fresh Start

"Every new party, every new bunch of people, and I start thinking that maybe this is my chance. That I am going to be normal again. A new leaf. A fresh start. But then I find myself at the party, thinking, oh, Yeah. This again."
Carol Rifka Brunt
Tell the Wolves I'm Home

In the years following my missed opportunity to achieve greatness in the entertainment (carnival) industry, the Street Kid was fervently attending classes in "Classical Failure," in preparation for the future as my Wisdom Teacher.

My teenage years were dominated by pretending to be an adult in situations in which I felt insecure or afraid, which was most of the time. In my thirteen-year-old mind, becoming an adult represented true freedom, and I felt that once I reached my twenties, I wouldn't have to pretend anymore. I didn't know it by the time I actually reached that milestone, but there were a few underlying issues that would sabotage my maturation for a long time to come, as I often seemed to think and act more like an errant child, rather than a responsible adult.

Moonlight in Mud Puddles

I celebrated my twentieth birthday by being homeless on the streets of Seattle again, but I didn't stay long. I was convinced that I could get a high-paying position in sales anytime, anywhere, if only they would interview me so I could help them match their needs with my abilities.

All I really needed was a fresh start—again.

After a few weeks of trying to put my life back together, I met a guy I had known before who offered a couch and a car to help me look for work.

———⋘⋙———

One morning as I was driving my friend's car out of the alley onto Pike Street, a car with four guys turned left into the alley coming toward me. Without enough room for both cars to pass, and since I was much closer to the street, I motioned to them to back up a few feet to let me out. The driver of the car flipped me off and yelled out the window,

"Back up F----er."

I looked behind me and realized that I would have to back up for half a city block to the entrance of the parking lot from which I had just emerged. Thinking I could reason with the driver better if we talked face-to-face, I walked up to his side of the car.

I had been eating a sweet roll for breakfast and was still munching on it when I approached the car.

I started to calmly explain my reasoning as to the logistics of his backing up a few feet to let me pass.

I said, "Sir, if you would be willing…" *when suddenly, I threw the sweet roll overhand at him. It exploded all over his*

32

face. I yelled, "What did you call me?"

He looked extremely shocked and quickly backed up, exclaiming, "I'm sorry, I'm sorry."

As I turned back to my car, I asked myself, *What in the world just happened? You attacked four guys in a car with a sweet roll? What would you have done if they misinterpreted your gesture of kindness and all jumped out to confront you?*

As I drove out, I didn't glance over to see if they had changed their minds, and so—trembling inside—I turned onto Pike Street and went on my way.

I suddenly had a flash in my mind of a headline from the *Seattle Times* :

Crazy twenty-year-old man attacks four University of Washington football players with a sweet roll and is stomped to death in response.

Kedric

Hey, man, we need to talk. What in the world made you think you could get away with that?

Doc

To tell the truth, it just happened. I guess I threw it before I had a chance to think at all.

Kedric

Oh, you didn't think first? Well, I think that's what's called a *no-brainer*.

Doc

Yeah, Impulsivity. Sometimes I still need to work on that.

Moonlight in Mud Puddles

After reframing the incident in my mind to become my heroic act of bravery by saving a child's life from being run over by a car with four Mafia hitmen using my French pastry to blind the perpetrators, I began to question my actions:

This isn't the first time that my temper has exploded from out of nowhere.

I wonder why?

What have I got to be mad about?

My life is finally getting on track.

I'm staying with my new best friend and his wife, so I have a warm couch and good food. Got an old car for a few more weeks, until I can get one of my own.

Just got a job selling an advertising package where I'm going to pull down big money any day now.

Nope, nothing that I've got to be upset about.

Now that I think about it, I won't be having any more outbursts like that.

I'm glad that's over.

My anger wasn't the only thing that was quick and explosive in those days. I also went through jobs like I was on a spy mission from an alien society that wanted to know the inner workings of the entire job market from Advertising to Zephyr Maintenance.

I was well on my way through the alphabet when I got to P for Pianos.

Having blown the advertising position (although it was actually a job selling sewing machines and cookware) because of a physical altercation with another salesman, I set out to find a more lucrative position suited to my talents.

As I walked past the huge music store on First Avenue called Sherman Clay, I impulsively walked inside and asked a clerk if they knew of any sales positions open?

The store was huge, with a large variety of musical instruments including pianos and organs.

I started talking to a salesman while the clerk went to find the manager.

"My dad is an orchestra conductor, and I was raised in a musical family," I told my captive audience, although I wasn't sure how this would help to get a sales position. "I play the trombone and even took a few piano lessons."

The salesman was looking at me as though I had suddenly grown a third eye in the middle of my forehead, when the clerk approached and stated, "They would like to see you upstairs for an interview."

As I followed her into a large area of offices, I wondered if I was stepping into a world of possibilities or another place of problems where I would be rejected once they found out about my true identity.

The door at the end of the hall said, "Al Stinson, Vice-President."

Inside the office, a tall, gray-haired man in an elegant suit greeted me warmly and offered me a chair.

"So, you are looking for a sales position. Do you

think you could sell pianos and organs?"

I nodded affirmatively as he continued speaking.

"Just this morning the manager of our piano store in Bremerton turned in his keys and quit saying, 'Nobody in Bremerton even wants a piano, and if they did, they wouldn't buy one from us.'"

The vice-president had my attention. He continued, "I was just debating whether we should close the store when I got word that a young man downstairs was asking about a job."

Mr. Stinson came out from behind his desk and sat on the chair next to me. He went on to say, "I am the vice-president of one of the largest music store chains in the world, responsible for sales and marketing for all of our stores on the west coast.

"Ric, the timing of this is so incredible; I am willing to take a chance on you as a complete unknown, to see if this store can be turned around. "We would have to give you some training for a week or so, but if you could begin to make a profit within a few months, your future would be ensured, and you could name your place with Sherman Clay!"

Without hesitation, I accepted the challenge and stated, "You won't be disappointed, sir."

After actually flying with me to Portland, Oregon, for a few days of personal training on selling the Lowrey organ, "Al," as I had come to know him, took me on Friday morning to visit my new store. It had been five days since I first walked into his office.

Bremerton, Washington, was reached from Seattle by

an hour ride across Puget Sound on one of the Washington State Ferries.

Al showed me the store, handed me the keys, and said, "Be here to open on Monday morning. Good luck!"

As I walked around inside my new store, I found a few dollars which I thought would be nice for the weekend's celebration and took the ferry back to downtown Seattle, where I was staying in my friend's apartment on Pike Street.

Monday morning, I missed the early ferry and showed up two hours late to find a chain and padlock across the front door.

When I called Al to find out how to get in, he replied, "Come on back to my office. We need to talk."

As I walked into the office, an old familiar feeling of disaster was creeping into my mind. Al started speaking, "One week ago a unique set of circumstances brought you to my door. After giving you the opportunity of a lifetime, this morning brings another unique set of circumstances. At eight o'clock this morning, one of our accountants went to the Bremerton store to do an audit so you could start business transactions. That accountant found the store locked with no manager present, and to top it off, found money missing from petty cash."

I started to protest that I had just barely missed the early ferry, but Al interrupted,

"I don't care if you took the money, but not being able to show up on time for your first day of work is inexcusable. I am sorry, but we are terminating your position and your future with Sherman Clay."

Moonlight in Mud Puddles

As I left the store and walked into the cold drizzle of a wet, gloomy Seattle day, I thought to myself, *Who cares! Seattle is just not the place for me. Imagine being in a situation where something as absurd as missing a ferry boat costs an entire career. The only thing good about Seattle is eating fish and chips at Ivar's. Someday I'm going to come back to Seattle after I'm successful and buy as much fish and chips as I want!*

It doesn't get any better than this!

Shortly after this my new best friend suggested that it was time for me to find a new place to crash and—disgusted—I agreed and hitchhiked back to my mother's house in Montana.

In a couple of weeks, I walked into Harold's Music Store in Great Falls, Montana, looking for a job. When they asked about experience, I told them that I had been the manager of a piano store in Bremerton, Washington, for Sherman Clay, and further that I had specialized training in selling the Lowery Organ!

They hired me on the spot....

I stayed at Harold's for longer than I had stayed anywhere since moving to Seattle after the sixth grade...a little over six months. The first week I sold six Baldwin pianos and one Lowrey organ and was informed that I was the top salesman for the Baldwin Piano Company that week nationwide.

I soon had a new set of clothes, a cool apartment of my own and had talked Harold into co-signing for a new car...a 1966 Mercury Cyclone GT with a 390 cubic inch engine. It was canary yellow with white pearl interior and black racing stripes down both sides.

I was finally reaching the potential people had told me about for years, and I was ready to make some serious life changes.

However, I was still lying to people about my past, and it started getting more and more difficult to keep up the facade.

My job was easy. I loaded pianos on the truck to take on the road responding to people who had expressed an interest in repossessed pianos. At that time, nobody seemed to want to pay a fair price for a new piano, so we sold new ones as repossessed in order to give people the deal they wanted. The rationale was that we were giving them the best deal possible, but they wanted more, so we lied to them in order to give them what they wanted.

The last straw for me was in the home of a young couple who were saving money to adopt a child. The wife had always dreamed of having a nice piano in her home, and once we unloaded it into her living room (just to see how it looked) both she and her husband argued back and forth about which choice they should make. My mind was screaming, *Don't take it. You can always get another piano, but this is about an unwanted child who needs your home to have a future!*

As I suggested that we load it back on the truck, the husband made a decision and wrote out a check for the full amount of the new, "repossessed" piano. I left them in conflict; the wife excited about her piano; the husband wondering if they had done the right thing.

Moonlight in Mud Puddles

My skill as a deceptive street hustler made me an excellent salesman.

It also made me sick.

I felt better on the streets; at least there, my scams wouldn't devastate the lives of unwanted children. So, I flipped the switch in my mind, went back to the store in Great Falls, got my pay and ran away from my feelings again.

The problem with handling feelings by "flipping a switch" and pretending they don't exist is that it becomes progressively easier to do that with all complications.

People who consciously or unconsciously shut off bad memories and feelings eventually lose the ability to feel the good ones, too.

To be in a state of numbness where the pain doesn't hurt is to also be in a fog, where navigation through life becomes hazardous.

After being sickened by my ability to convince the young couple to choose the piano rather than the child, I went back to stay at my mother's house in Helena, Montana, to regroup. I was tired of being a hustler who had no purpose or meaning in life, so I started looking for a "working man's job" to move my career opportunities in a more wholesome direction.

I became friends with a disc jockey who did a music and talk show on the radio for a local station in Helena. Danny had a golden baritone voice, was 6'4" tall, with dark skin and jet black hair. He had a way with women, and many of them hung around the radio station to meet him just because of his voice. When they saw him, they offered to pay his way, just for the chance to be with him.

I started thinking that maybe I also could become a D.J. because my voice was somewhat like Danny's, even though I was fairly sure the outcome with women would be different once they saw me. I was almost twenty-one years old, and Danny was around thirty, so I figured with more time and training by an expert, I could at least perfect the radio gig, if not the social aspect.

Danny, on the other hand, was tired of women "bugging" him because of his job. He would often say, "I like to pick my own dates, but when they come to the station to meet me, they are usually hard up, unattractive, and think I want to go with them because they have money.

"I can't tell them to bug off, because the radio station wants me to be nice for public relations. I feel like a cheap prostitute!"

I was not as opposed to either position, as a D.J., loved for my voice, or being paid for party favors, but thought I might be humiliated if one of them wanted to pay me by asking if I had change for a quarter.

At that point in my life, my self-esteem was pretty low often viewing myself as "big, dumb, and stupid-looking."

Danny and I were shooting pool in a local pub, one day, when we met some guys who were linemen for Western Union. They were traveling as a crew taking down wire from telephone poles across Montana and would stay in motels in nearby cities while they went out following train tracks and highways to remove the wires.

Moonlight in Mud Puddles

One of the pool shooters was the crew chief, who assured us they had a couple of positions open, and in addition to our pay, we would receive a daily allowance for food and lodging.

"That sounds awesome," we both agreed. "What are the duties?"

The crew chief said, "In addition to the care and moving of the vehicles and equipment, all you have to do is climb 45-foot telephone poles and loosen the wire to be reeled up by trucks that are following the crew."

Immediately both Danny and I agreed that we felt a calling to be linemen and would leave Helena the following week when the crew moved to Drummond, Montana, for the next section. We were advanced funds to buy work clothes and steel-toed boots and were told we would pay for them over several weeks' pay.

I was excited about being on a work crew where I would not be required to be deceptive or hustle anybody out of anything—except—there was no way I was going to climb one of those telephone poles.

Since the time I fell down a cargo hold in the Navy a few years before, I had become terrified of heights, especially if I was just a few feet off the ground with nothing between me and the deck below. Of course, I didn't share that with anybody on the crew, because we were a rough and ready, macho group who could just as easily be called by the military to jump out of an airplane on a secret rescue mission in Vietnam.

When we got to Drummond, we had a couple of days to relax over the weekend before going to work on

42

Monday, so after checking into our motel, we headed downtown to a bar with pool tables.

I usually fit in well with people playing pool because it was one skill I had become fairly proficient at since my time on the streets. In the bar, there happened to be another line crew for Northern Pacific Railroad, and they challenged us to play for drinks.

We were all getting pretty drunk, when someone from the other crew suggested, "You guys are pretty okay at pool, but how are you at climbing poles? Let's have a race!"

There was a pole by the station in the center of town which was much taller than the rest. The most experienced lineman from each crew was selected, and we all went to the station to watch. Our man went first, climbing with his safety belt around the pole, pulling it up with him as he took huge steps, racing up the wooden pole. He almost slipped on his descent, but the safety strap caught him. His time was just under 15 seconds, and we were all cheering and celebrating because we thought we would win.

The Northern Pacific guy was preparing to go and decided that the safety strap would just delay his time, so he started racing up without it. He went up much faster than our crew member and reached the top in record time.

Just as he started down, his foot slipped, and leaning back as though the strap would catch him, he fell to the concrete platform below.

Somebody yelled, "Don't move him."

43

Moonlight in Mud Puddles

As we waited for the ambulance, we covered him with a blanket and watched in silence as the life drained out of him.

As I watched, his left hand twitched a little, and I noticed a plain gold wedding band on his ring finger. I thought about his wife alone and maybe little children without a dad, just because of a stupid challenge to prove which drunken climber was faster.

At that moment, I knew I would never be a lineman.

On Monday morning, as Danny and I were to start our training, I couldn't get the image of the lineman's wedding band out of my mind, especially after we learned he had been pronounced dead at the hospital. Danny climbed his short practice pole without any hitch, and everybody cheered him on for completing this "rite of passage" and welcoming him as a member of the crew. Then it was my turn. I got about five feet up when my legs began shaking uncontrollably, and I could barely make it down without falling.

I "tried" a couple more times that week, but it soon became apparent that I would not make it, and when they moved to Missoula the next week, I was off the crew. I didn't even get to keep my boots.

A few years later, I found out that Danny was working on wire take-down in the same area, touched a wire that wasn't supposed to be hot and was electrocuted.

The week after I arrived in Missoula, I got a job selling shoes at OGG shoe store downtown on Higgins Avenue. I made a career decision to stay there forever and eventually open my own store—*except*—after doing great for a week, I celebrated my twenty-first birthday by staying up until five A.M. When I called in and was honest about why I missed the next day, I was terminated over the phone.

I went back to my mother's house in Helena to rest before my next escapade.

———

Watching the lineman die was a pivotal event in my life. Since the time I was thirteen-years-old, I had many moments in which I felt I had nothing left to live for. But after watching him die, I felt exhausted with the futility of life.

I couldn't seem to break the pattern of starting well yet finishing disastrously. It was never my intention to fail so badly or so often, but I couldn't get a handle to put the brakes on my rapid descent into the abyss. My future looked bleak, yet somehow I still had a flicker of hope that something would happen to bring the change that was so badly needed.

I had no idea that in a few years when it actually happened, it would be accompanied by so much more chaos!

4

The Misfit

"There's a race of men that don't fit in,
a race that can't stay still.
So they break the hearts of kith and kin,
and they roam the world at will."
Robert Service
The Men that Don't Fit In

Over the years I have worked with a lot of teenagers, and adults, too, who are often bewildered by their own inexplicable behavior. Referred to therapy by parents, teachers, etc., who themselves are completely frustrated, I often hear, "I don't understand. I have provided every opportunity for this kid to get it together; it seems like all they want to do is be angry and sullen. If you can't fix this kid, then I'm giving up!"

As a family therapist, I wish part of the requirement for "fixing the kid" would be mandatory sessions for the adults who are most frustrated by the actions of the child. In cases where the adults are actively involved in the treatment plan, all participants are encouraged to view themselves as part of a system of healing, rather

Moonlight in Mud Puddles

than focusing only on the "problem child." Each member must be part of the "treatment team" and as such, be willing to engage in the change process for all concerned.

Unfortunately, most schools, teachers, and parents in society are geared to rewarding the well-behaved model child, while the rebellious misfit is removed from the learning atmosphere to make room for the more conforming, obedient, well-behaved protégé with such a bright future.

However, as Nobel Prize-winning author, Hermann Hesse, proclaims in *Beneath the Wheel,*

> *"Time and again the ones who are detested by their teachers and frequently punished, the runaways and those expelled, are the ones who afterwards add to society's treasure…. Thus the struggle between rule and spirit repeats itself year after year from school to school."*

As an educator myself, I certainly understand how disruptive a difficult student can be in a classroom setting. However, isolation and expulsion would be the last resort by the teacher and administrator well-trained in encouraging troubled kids. If I hope to help troubled kids, I must encourage them to attempt something which is terrifying…to be open and vulnerable. Of course, encouraging vulnerability in troubled kids is impossible without a willingness and commitment to engage in being open and vulnerable to oneself. That is one of the most powerful and rewarding things about being a therapist to troubled people: If you are going to help others, you have to keep working on your own stuff!

The "Sweet Roll" incident is one example of stuff I have to keep working on. Of course, it happened a *few* years ago at the age of twenty when I was homeless and penniless on the streets of Seattle, but regardless of any real or imagined contributing factors, I can never get better if I'm not willing to face my darkest places.

My *Intermittent Explosive Disorder* as described in the *Diagnostic and Statistical Manual of Mental Disorders* comes from the darkest and most distant places of my soul. Anger is easy to bury because it blocks out almost all other feelings until something triggers it. My sudden explosive anger often erupted when I least expected, giving the impression that it had a will of its own. The truth, however, is that my anger kept me safe on the streets. It became almost an autonomic response when the street kid within sensed danger or felt threatened in some way.

The anger usually stayed just beneath the surface, waiting to rear its ugly head if anyone or anything strayed too close. Unfortunately, it also became extremely self-destructive. Rather than protecting me from harm, my explosive anger often placed me in a dangerous situation, like the sweet roll attack, where a cool head may have prevailed, thereby actually averting the crisis.

As described in *Wisdom from the Streets,*

"My own self-image, my deep-seated anger, and my street persona as a manipulative, tough-guy hustler have served to derail my best intentions on numerous occasions."

Research in Social Psychology suggests that when people are confronted with a situation in which they feel a loss of control, they will shift into an emotional state like anger, because anger is much more desirable than fear or guilt. This is one reason that abused children regardless of age act out in destructive behavior when they feel fear, shame, or guilt. Smashing things or yelling at someone produces a much greater feeling of control than being in trouble and not knowing what's coming next.

It's just so hard to be real when I feel like I'm in trouble most of the time. I have the strangest feeling that if something is wrong, it must be my fault. Some people say that I "must have a guilty conscience," but I don't have to feel guilty or even have done something wrong to feel that trouble is coming.

In many years of working with troubled kids, I realize that they, like myself, often have no idea why they are in trouble—no idea why they smashed their favorite and most treasured possessions, or why they can't remember what they did, why they got angry or ran away. So often when pressured by authority figures such as teachers, probation/police officers, and parents, etc. to tell them, "Why did you do that?"—the child faces a terrible dilemma. "If I tell the truth, which is that *I don't know*, they just believe that I'm rebellious and unwilling to change—and that makes me even more angry!"

Looking deep within to the hidden places where the anger resides gives me the opportunity to choose self-control if I become empowered enough to be real with myself.

It is not easy.

———

One of the experiences that brought a clear demonstration of anger control happened when I was a bouncer in a night club in my early twenties. The club had two primary bartenders who were both purported to have mysterious and felonious backgrounds. One of them had already revealed to me that he had been incarcerated in the federal penitentiary at McNeil Island near Tacoma. The other bartender was muscular, sinister and often aloof when I tried to engage him in conversation.

One day after I had commented on something that he was ignoring, I goaded him to respond by stating, "I hope what I said didn't make you mad."

He turned toward me, and with a cold, cynical look that froze me in my tracks said, "What in the world would make you think that someone like you could ever make me mad?"

The next thought in my head was *choose your next words carefully* as I suddenly had a strong awareness that I was on shaky ground and dangerous footing. I wisely decided to keep still, and turning around, went about my business.

This man's powerful edict was a life-changing revelation that remains to this day. I was painfully aware that his self-control, his self-awareness, and his complete detachment, indicated that if he was going to be angry, it would be because he chose to do so, not because anybody could make him.

Moonlight in Mud Puddles

After years of emulating this truth—and also many times of trial and error—I now believe I am secure enough within myself to proclaim, "There is not a living human being that can make me mad...only I can choose to do so...and I don't choose to give anyone that power over me!"

Self-control is a tremendous motivation that has the potential to set me free from my own self-destructive compulsions...and even propel me towards success.

Of course, as a "mature" adult who often has the emotions and reactions of a thirteen-year-old, I have experienced the outburst more times than I would like to remember.

At least, I never used a sweet roll again.

My immersion into the music business is a glaring example of using my street skills to present myself at the top of my game, regardless of my ability to do much other than be deceptive. Like my anger, deception seemed to burst forth in any situation in which I felt in danger of exposure. Even though I was a "mature" adult at the age of twenty, when I walked into Sherman Clay in Seattle, things just seemed to go better, at least initially, if I told those people what they wanted to hear. I felt like I couldn't be honest about who and what I really was, anyway.

As stated in *Wisdom from the Streets,* "I also learned to survive by lying. It was called hustling, and I hustled every person and in every way that I could."

As a therapist working in both residential treatment for troubled teenagers and also in private practice specializing in issues of the dysfunctional family system, I have worked with a lot of people who have problems with deception. Many of them really don't want to lie in situations that may simply invite more chaos, but they have learned by personal experience that telling the truth, the whole truth, and nothing but the truth brings more problems with others who are judgmental and punitive, regardless of the relationship, even within their own family.

Probing underneath the deception often reveals a person who is terrified of themselves and their hidden compulsions, and lying keeps the inevitable doom from crashing down upon them, if only for a little while. Throughout my years of working with troubled families and kids, I often heard the axiom that *children don't lie about abuse* or the hidden things that happen to them in the dysfunctional family.

In my experience, however, the truth is that children do lie, but *they lie to get out of trouble, not to get into trouble.* In my case, I *lied* to *hide*, because a lie is often the nearest exit from an adolescent dilemma. At the root of all my lying and hiding was a *fear* of everything.

I was afraid of:

- **Exposure**—as the street kid whose self-image even as an adult subconsciously declared that I was like a leper in ancient lands who truly needed to loudly proclaim that I was "Unclean!" and any contact with the "real me" would end in disastrous consequences.

- **Isolation and Alienation**—because I knew that I didn't belong anywhere in the pretend world that I manufactured to hide my true identity. Thus every waking moment embraced an identity that left me alone anyway.

- **Verbal and Physical Violence**—as stated in *Wisdom From the Streets,* "To survive on the streets, I faked being a bad, tough guy—nobody to mess with, somebody to be left alone." But inside, even though I rarely allowed myself to be aware of my feelings, I was terrified in any situation in which I felt threatened—which was most of the time.

- **Discovery**—that I was mentally retarded and physically challenged and in any encounter that led to an actual confrontation, I would be as vulnerable as "Slimy Slim" in the county jail in Salem, Oregon.

The physical and emotional violence of my stepfather and the sexual encounter with the older woman left me with traumatic, conflicting emotions of failure and inadequacy. I secretly wanted to be accepted and loved by everybody I met, yet regularly hid behind a facade of aloofness and drove others away at the slightest hint of rejection. Wanting to be loved by anyone, I pushed everyone away. I was an emotional basket-case.

As a result, without even being aware of it, I became

an *approval junkie.* I wanted everyone else to know that I really wasn't what I believed myself to be, and so without realizing it at the time, I tried to impress everybody by my knowledge of life through an incessant stream of verbosity. In other words, I talked all the time about almost anything, regardless of the subject matter or interest to the listener. I just wanted them to like me. I wanted them to be impressed. It usually backfired.

As the primary teacher, Dr. Aarhus, at the Vancouver Boy's Academy often said to me, "Do you have to tell everything you know?"

In hindsight, I realized he was urging me to shut up, listen, and maybe even learn something, but back then I just thought that he was impressed with my knowledge, and I became even more astute at expressing myself in his presence.

Kedric

So, you wanted his approval, but talked so much, that you talked your way out of it?

Doc

You know, I might be better off if you quit talking to me!

Kedric

How would I learn anything? The voice in my head always gives me a new perspective. Thanks, Doc.

Doc

Just keep listening.

Moonlight in Mud Puddles

An *approval junkie* is someone who becomes addicted to the praise of others. Not having a self-image which stands alone on its own merit, the approval junkie thrives on the appreciation of performance regardless of how menial the task, in hopes of feeling good about themselves even for a fleeting moment. But as in all addictions, no amount of the drug is ever enough.

The codependent is like the sister to the approval junkie. When codependents have a headache, they look for someone else who may need an aspirin. Unable to meet their own needs, they are only allowed to treat themselves after being reassured that no one else needs the aspirin at that moment more than they do. Once satisfied that the imminent needs of everybody else are met—often after much reassurance—they become free to treat themselves for the moment. Like the codependent, an approval junkie is suffering from an insidious addiction that will destroy everything in their lives.

Allowing everybody else's opinion of your performance to be the primary source of how you feel about yourself is a ticket to personal deprivation and desolation.

For many years—even into adulthood—I was an "approval junkie"—but with a twist: I wanted everyone to like me, but pushed them away as soon as possible, because I knew that once my initial amazing performance was finished, they would see my true self and reject me.

———❦———

There was a time in my life that I enjoyed my own company and, as an imaginative child, loved playing for hours alone as a member of King Arthur's Round Table of exemplary knights; and sometimes the first mate on a pirate ship named the Jolly Roger. But all that ended abruptly when I became a street kid who tried to put up a good front but needed the approval of almost everyone just to make it through the day. Between wanting the approval of others to feel good about myself, yet often surrounded by people whose expectations I could never meet—it became apparent that no amount of approval or performance would ever make me good enough for others—or myself.

The addiction to my approval fix became almost as strong as my need to run away. I lived in a self-defeating cycle of seeking approval, even by helping others, yet ready to run away at a moment's notice if someone's response hurt my feelings or threatened my existence in some unimaginable way.

Even as a therapist, I often felt I could help others become more self-empowered to break negative patterns, while truly blind to some of my own addictive issues.

The pathway out requires that I confront myself in the mirror of my memory, and without self-condemnation or judgments, face the feelings that I have tried so hard to avoid. I love the axiom: Get **Sad,** not **Mad**!

Getting underneath to the frightened child within is a difficult yet truly rewarding process. As I gain self-esteem and self-control over my need to cover my feelings with anger, deception, or pathologically pleasing others, I can *feel,* rather than *run* from sadness and pain.

Moonlight in Mud Puddles

No matter how uncomfortable my insecure self, I can pay attention to the message they bring and use the wisdom to keep getting healthy.

Being released from the incessant need to be angry or deceptive or seeking approval allows me to examine my underlying motivation and change direction. I become free to choose where, when, and how to meet my needs as well as those of others, thus pursuing a greater path of peace and harmony with all things. I now am empowered to celebrate my *Be-ing,* rather than my *Do-ing,* and once again become the creative, imaginative boy who sometimes thinks I may actually be on the wisdom staff in King Arthur's court—or at the helm of the Jolly Roger—and loving every moment exploring the Magic of Life!

5
Transfiguration

"The beauty that emerges from woundedness is a beauty infused with feeling, a beauty different from the beauty of landscape and the cold perfect form. This is a beauty that has suffered its way through the ache of desolation until the words or music emerged to equal the hunger and desperation at its heart... Where woundedness can be refined into beauty a wonderful transfiguration takes place."
John O'Donohue
Beauty: The Invisible Embrace

The lineman continued to haunt me. It wasn't just his violent death that penetrated my thoughts—but his life. I often visualized him with a wife and child, and the potential of a bright future with all the hopes and dreams available in life—gone in one disastrous impulsive moment. I knew nothing about him, but because of the many disastrous consequences of my own impulsive moments, instead of the lineman, I saw myself lying on the ground.

By the time I reached the ripe old age of twenty-four, having already lived several lifetimes in a single decade,

Moonlight in Mud Puddles

I had decided that I'd had enough. I had been living in Missoula, Montana for a couple of years, taking a few classes at the University of Montana, bartending at a local rock & roll nightclub and experimenting with L.S.D., Mescaline, and a variety of drugs. With little motivation to succeed at any endeavor, after lifetimes of failure, it seemed that as my drug use accelerated my life completely faltered.

As I had so often in my troubled existence, I just wanted to give up because I had nothing left to live for. It seemed that nothing I had ever done had any meaning or purpose other than to send me into a dark abyss with the only light illuminating every failure in exquisite detail. After each thought of dark despair rose the image of the lineman lying on the ground. I knew in my heart that even though I felt desperate, I didn't want to end up the same way. In the Vancouver Boys' Academy at fifteen years old, I had been strongly influenced by the Christian faith of staff members who were able to set aside their doctrinal differences in order to help kids whose lives were shattered. I always wanted what it seemed the academy staff experienced, so I turned to religion.

One Sunday morning, I impulsively went to a nearby church with a couple of friends who were also curious about the supernatural. The pastor and several friendly parishioners descended on us immediately after the service, quizzing us about our beliefs, and then to soften the inquisition, invited us to lunch. Pastor Carl Perry of the

60

"Assembly Of God" church was actually quite friendly and seemed interested in us beyond the obvious motive of gaining new converts to the faith.

He gave us all copies of a book called *The Cross and the Switchblade* about a young minister who worked with street kids in New York City. He also told us that the author, David Wilkerson, was coming to Missoula in two weeks, and invited us to the event. After I started reading it, I couldn't put it down and read it all the way through in one sitting. I called the pastor and told him it was my intention to attend the youth crusade meeting on the second of the two nights because I had to bartend the first, but I assured him I would go if for no other reason than to meet the author of such an inspirational book.

At the close of the meeting, Rev. Wilkerson asked anyone that needed new hope in their lives to join him at the front. I went forward and "gave my heart to the Lord."

Although I no longer view spirituality as confined to any specific religion, the spiritual change seemed instantaneous and intense. Later in writing about the experience, I said, "The only way I could express the magnitude of that moment was in the terms of the feeling that swept over me. I felt an immediate rush of peace and tranquility, coupled with an awareness of a love so total and complete that I burst into tears at the realization of its beauty."

I really did feel different in the core of my being. My life had new motivation, and now I wondered if I could, maybe, help others instead of lying to them to further my selfish purposes. Immediately after the meeting, I felt a strong urge to approach David Wilkerson and tell him that I wanted to come to visit his work with street kids in New York, and even though I only had enough money to just get there, I wanted to come as soon as possible.

Reverend Wilkerson took me into a side room, and told me, "It's one in a thousand, but the Lord is impressing me to invite you to come right away. I will keep you for a week, show you the work we have throughout the city, and then I will personally pay your way back."

I flew to New York City three days later, had an amazing experience visiting the "Teen Challenge" ministries as described in *The Cross and the Switchblade,* and then took the bus back to Montana.

On the bus, I met a traveling minister who planted an idea in my mind of using my street background to start work in Missoula for young people who were hooked on drugs and needed to be set free.

Pastor Perry picked me up at the bus station, with several new friends, and we all went out to eat. I was excited about my entire trip, but mostly shared about the inspiration of meeting the traveling minister on the bus and the idea of starting some kind of work with young people in Missoula struggling with drug addictions and wasted lives.

After I got home and had a good night's sleep, I woke up at 8:00 am with my mind racing about finding a place in Missoula to help troubled kids. Immediately, I went to my kitchen table and started writing ideas down, which seemed to flow as if I was merely a scribe writing down the words of another. I wrote down the plans for a house, which could contain a coffee-house ministry and a drop-in center for counseling, somewhere in the vicinity of the university to be available to needy students. I then wrote plans for an advisory board from the pastors of different churches in order to facilitate city-wide partic-ipation. When I finished writing, I felt that I should call the pastor and tell him about my ideas.

It was 9:00 Monday morning, and realizing it was likely the pastor's day off, I called his home apologeti-cally.

"Sorry to bother you, Pastor Perry, but I really need to come talk to you."

He responded, "I know, come on over."

Bewildered by his comment, I wondered what I was getting myself into, but decided to make a brief visit to share my idea. When I got to his house, the living room was full of people.

The pastor introduced me as, "Ric Cecil, who has just returned from spending a week in New York City with David Wilkerson and Teen Challenge. Ric, tell us about your experience in New York..."

I responded, "Pastor, I'd like to tell you about that, but I've got to tell you about this other thing first."

As soon as I got the words out of my mouth, the peo-ple in the room erupted in prayer and praise, which sur-prised and scared me into thinking I wanted to run out the door.

Moonlight in Mud Puddles

When the commotion in the room died down, the Pastor turned to me and said, "At four o'clock this morning I was awakened with a vision that Ric Cecil was going to call me at nine a.m. to talk about starting a work for needy young people in Missoula. The Lord showed me how the initial conversation would go with my asking about New York, and you responding that you had to tell me about this other thing first.

"I felt that I should call my ministerial staff, board members, and youth leaders, who were sitting here waiting for your call at 9:00 a.m."

The crazy thing is that he knew *four hours* before I did that I was coming to see him.

Kedric

I guess you know that's Unbelievable...maybe even Impossible.

Doc

What else is new? But the cool thing is that because it's true, it is overflowing with lessons for life in every way imaginable!

Because of the radical change in my life, I was soon speaking to packed churches who were eager to hear about this miraculous conversion experience. Many people were warm and supportive as I tried to be open about my transformative change, even though I saw some similarities to piano sales with people coming to hear the "good news" without wanting to hear about the struggles and failures.

Within two weeks of my experience, I was the founder and director of a drop-in center and coffee-house ministry, reaching out to young people looking for a change. We named it "Challenge House." We had pastors from different Christian churches on the Board of Directors, giving credence and guidance as the ministry received donations from the community.

The "challenge" became my total inability to do anything other than put up a good front. On the surface, I was able to blend my street skills into my enthusiasm for spiritual transformation. I was ready to save others who were drowning like I had been. Saving me from chaos in my new administrative role would be something else entirely.

———

While speaking to a packed house at a local church in Missoula, I had an experience that shook me to the core—and was only a foreshadow of the chaos to come. As I stood at the pulpit, dressed in my new silver-gray suit (like James Bond wore) with my raspberry-colored shirt and matching tie, I felt confident that the standing-room-only-filled church would be richly blessed by my performance as I told the story of the pastor's vision and the miraculous events surrounding it all.

I had shared the story in several churches and was getting a lot of approval from many listeners and willing participants in the project. On this occasion, when I began to speak, I experienced what I now know was my first panic attack. I felt nervous and started sweating profusely. I became terrified that I was unable to say more than a few sentences, which didn't even seem to be connected. I felt like I was losing control of my mind and my words and just wanted to run out of the room screaming.

The pastor was a nice guy named Dan, who brought me a glass of water, and encouraged me to "relax and take my time."

Suddenly, a woman stood up in the middle of the fourth row on my left side, pointed her finger at me and loudly exclaimed, "Ric Cecil, I don't know you at all, but I believe you have become conceited about all that is happening as though it's all about you instead of the miraculous power of God!"

As I looked at her, everyone and everything seemed to vanish from view, as her words jolted me back into a reality that I didn't want to face. In spite of everything that had happened in just a few short weeks, I was still just a misfit. I suddenly felt naked and exposed in front of God and everybody—and just wanted to run back into the darkest alley I could find.

I responded, "I believe you are right."

The anxiety passed, and I was able to finish the message, but this was the beginning of the end. I began to feel that I was in way over my head with the demands of everything. I started looking for a way out.

Within a few months, I was burnt out by trying to put it all together. I had gone from dark to light in 2.3 seconds, and the change was too much to handle. Suffering from emotional overload, it was decided that I would attend Trinity Bible College in North Dakota for training and much-needed grounding.

Challenge House was placed under the leadership of a young man who was an ordained minister, to continue the work, and I packed my few belongings and headed out of town.

When I arrived at the school, I had a nervous breakdown, and that became the start of an amazing journey of transformation unlike anything I could imagine, as the Street Kid, the Misfit tried to conform into the image of a good conservative, Bible-believing, fundamentalist, victorious Christian. But all my skill to put up a good front completely vanished, as every moment was dominated by an almost indescribable preoccupation with apprehension and fear.

I had an anxiety disorder, twenty-four hours, seven days a week, with daily panic attacks. I found that I was too nervous to even engage in conversation, so I spent a lot of time alone. Well-meaning, concerned fellow students and staff often tried to encourage me by saying, "God doesn't want you to be sick, so let's pray together."

But I was sick, and nothing spiritual or magical made it better. I was sick, and even though I had experienced a miraculous conversion that demonstrated supernatural power beyond all natural explanations, I had blown it again. I was a misfit, and no matter what anyone be-

Moonlight in Mud Puddles

lieved, I would never be well, because...I was a Failure...a Street Kid that couldn't fit in no matter what I tried.

———————

Many people have asked what turned me around in the first place from a pathway of self-destruction, toward being able to offer help to others with similar issues. The answer is: In addition to a whole lot of life experiences that brought me to the brink of a disaster, I experienced *a touch of the miraculous from heaven and an anxiety disorder from hell!*

Every day was like living in a nightmare. I went to classes and tried to concentrate, but often felt like I just wanted to run out of the room screaming, "the sky is falling!" like *Chicken Little* of the classic fable who misinterprets a falling acorn for a piece of the sky and instantly experiences a full-blown panic attack. My thoughts and feelings were just as irrational, and I often felt like the world around me was going to crash on top of my head at any moment.

There just wasn't anywhere to run from the feelings of fear and insanity inside my head. Most of my classmates and teachers seemed to agree that my world was falling, and they not only couldn't relate or understand but gave me a lot of room just in case my fears would fall on them too.

Fortunately, there was one notable exception. One of my teachers, Paul Davidson, was open about his own anxiety disorder. "Brother" Davidson, as we all called him in the vernacular of the school, was an amazing man. He was given a desk, chair, and bed in the basement furnace room, and I spent many hours there in discussion with him. He often talked about feeling as though he couldn't explain to others what anxiety and panic felt like, but in me, he found a willing protégé who hung on his every word. He related how difficult it was to feel drained of energy throughout days filled with anxiety, yet be unable to sleep at night even though often exhausted.

"I just can't shut off my mind sometimes, with racing thoughts that seem so disconnected," he would say. "Sometimes it seems that nothing helps, except getting outside to go walking whenever I feel so anxious that I just can't stay still."

He encouraged me to walk everywhere I went, allowing my mind to be distracted by the world around me, instead of the incessant thoughts of impending doom.

Brother Davidson also talked about life experiences, which often made him feel like a misfit!

He shared, "I started two mission schools for children in the Philippines, but because of my caustic personality, the school boards eventually wouldn't allow me to teach in either one. One day as I was walking along a dirt road outside one of the schools, I saw a big dirt clod in the middle of the road and kicked it, exclaiming to myself, "That's you, Davidson; you're just a dirt clod that can't fit in with anybody or anything.

"The next day a torrential rain hit the area, and as I walked along in the same spot, the dirt clod was not only gone but blended together with everything as smooth as glass."

Moonlight in Mud Puddles

As he told the story, I saw myself as the dirt clod and understood the message.

The object lesson by this great teacher, who so often taught from the depths of his own humility, came through loud and clear. If I would submit to the forces, which were shaping my life instead of resisting everything, someday I too may be able to move in peace and harmony with the world around me.

This was the first time I caught the concept of "going with the flow." I was momentarily encouraged but felt as though it would take a flood of Biblical proportions to make me fit with others. Even Brother Davidson's attitude toward marriage made me feel further isolated. After sharing some of my background before my conversion experience, he stated to me, "When you attempt to find a soul mate to share your life, instead of picking someone who can't relate, *find someone that is as messed up as you are!*"

This stinging indictment seemed to discount my miraculous change into becoming "a new creation," and I often subconsciously attempted to do just the opposite, as I pursued partners who were nothing like me. However, after many years, failing to heed the advice of this wise sage, I now realize that he was speaking truth from the top of the mountain.

Unfortunately, I have never found anyone who fits that criteria.

Other than my time with Brother Davidson in the furnace room, the only time I felt a little bit of peace was walking alone in a nearby park. I learned to "stay in the moment," instead of obsessing about my tumultuous past or uncertain future. The trees offered a feeling of protection, becoming familiar friends, and the stream of water that slowly meandered through the park brought life to everything—including me—and slowly I began to emerge from my shell.

I took a job after school hours driving a taxi, and little by little, began to open up and connect with others again.

After a couple of years at Trinity, I was invited to speak at a banquet to help the Vancouver Boys Academy transition to several group homes called "Youth Outreach, Inc." After the banquet, I was asked to join the staff and started working in the group home program with troubled kids, just like I had been—and often still was. I stayed for 8 1/2 years. Being a staff member in the program where I had once been a resident was awesome. Now I just needed to face my own stuff, and I began to reflect on the underlying issues that had not been resolved with my spiritual change.

I still found that trying to put up a good front took the attention off me when I struggled with my new-found faith. I became aware that the street kid was constantly trying to avoid conflict by running away when others seemed displeased or disappointed because the wounds of my past often made it difficult to face things in their lives that triggered my pain. But I couldn't allow my stuff to get in the way of helping the kids, so I had to face my

Moonlight in Mud Puddles

pain, and taking one step at a time, continue the healing process.

I just wanted to be real: with the kids, with my co-workers, and with anybody who would listen. But I often found myself wanting to go home to the streets, back to the freedom of not having to face responsibility, especially where I could escape the biggest phony in the world...myself.

6

Even in This Darkness

"I know your soul is on life support and that you feel lost and like you're completely spinning out of control, but you're finding yourself – here, tonight... even in this darkness."
Jennifer Elisabeth
Born Ready: Unleash Your Inner Dream Girl

The first time I told a patient about my having an anxiety disorder with panic attacks, she exclaimed, "You? Are you kidding me? I thought I was the only one!"

The Diagnostic and Statistical Manual of Mental Disorders list of symptoms for *Generalized Anxiety Disorder* include,

> *"excessive worry and anxiety about a variety of topics, events, or activities, even when there is nothing wrong or in a manner which is disproportionate to the actual risk...A high percentage of waking hours worrying about something."*

Panic attacks are listed to include recurrent and unexpected numbness or tingling, heart palpitations, fear of losing control or dying, sweating, dizziness, trembling, fear of going crazy, feelings of unreality (derealization)

73

Moonlight in Mud Puddles

or detached from self (depersonalization).

A clinician can accurately diagnose the disorders from recognition of the criteria and symptoms being present in a patient for at least six months, but to experience them is almost indescribable...unless you've been there yourself.

When the symptoms initially appeared in my life, after I arrived at Trinity, I thought I was losing my mind and going completely crazy. The first time I went into a grocery store, I envisioned the checkout clerk staring at me because I was certain she "knew" something was wrong. I imagined that she was about to say, "are you all right? Do you need me to call an ambulance or something?"

If the line of people waiting was more than two or three people, the feelings of awareness built to a crescendo so intense that by the time it was my turn, I wanted to escape before they could call the police, put me in a straitjacket, and stick me away for the rest of my life.

I began avoiding lines and people in general. The food line in the cafeteria at Trinity was excruciating. I just couldn't stand there more than a few minutes. I began waiting until I thought everyone had gone through, but if the line was too long, I just skipped the meal entirely. Good nutrition or balanced meals were the last of my concern. Somehow, I just needed to eat something, and it was a good day when I was able to have at least one meal, but rarely two.

The basic tasks of life were almost impossible. Simply putting one foot in front of the other often required intense concentration, and I felt exhausted most of the time whether day or night.

I once told a friend that I had forgotten how to walk and running, was completely out of the question. Further, I tried to explain what it felt like trying to remember the mechanics of taking one step at a time. He simply substantiated my self-diagnosis by stating, "Sorry brother, but that sounds crazy!"

I stopped trying to explain the unexplainable to those who could never understand and retreated silently back into the chaos of my inner world.

***

I was somewhat better by the time I started working at Youth Outreach, Inc. in Vancouver, Washington; the program I was placed in as a ward of the court ten years before. Because of my personal history and religious conversion, I was viewed as a success story and given the task of trying to raise money for the cost of care.

Shortly after my arrival, the executive director (who had been my coach and mentor at the Vancouver Boys Academy) brought me into his well-appointed office and said, "Ric, it's great to have you on board. Now go out into the community, tell what the program has done for you, and ask people to give money to support the work."

As I left the office, my anxiety went through the roof as I realized I not only didn't have a clue of how to proceed but was still terrified of personal encounters with almost anybody. Images of the checkout clerk at the grocery store flooded my troubled mind, and I once again saw myself being hauled away to be locked up forever.

Without a car, I walked down the street near the office and went into a flower shop on the corner. The woman at the counter was serving a customer, and smiling at me, said, "I'll be with you in a moment."

She was the only employee in the little shop and seemed in a hurry and really busy. I felt like a grade schooler selling cookies for a class project who wanted to blurt out, "I'm selling cookies, and I'm pretty sure you don't want to buy any!"

After I started to tell her who I was, another customer walked in, and while I waited again, she suddenly reached in the till and handed me a five dollar bill, exclaiming, "I just don't have any time today, but I hope this helps a little!"

Somewhat stunned, I walked into the street thinking, "That wasn't so bad," and decided to try it again with other businesses on the street. By the end of the day, I had begun to overcome my fear and anxiety and had sixty dollars in my pocket.

Eventually, after several years as the Director of Development and Relief Houseparent for Youth Outreach, Inc., I was speaking on a regular basis to churches, Rotary and Kiwanis Clubs, and presenting our program to a network of business people, both locally and throughout the state of Washington.

As my confidence grew, the panic and anxiety became a distant memory. I began to feel empowered to pursue educational and other opportunities in our ever increasing work with troubled kids.

As a Family Therapist and University Professor, I have had many opportunities to relate to patients, and students in the throes of anxiety disorders and panic attacks. Often, like the first patient I told, they said, "Wow, it's so comforting to know that someone understands being trapped in the feelings of this nightmare."

"But what did it take to get better?"

Of course, the answer is, that because the anxiety disorders are always present in the memories and mindset of the subconscious, the healing process must be constant and can include many components. It may be facilitated by medication or mindfulness. We can participate in a variety of therapies and ideas which help us learn to relax, reframe our experiences, and relive our distress no matter what the reality that confronts us.

But ultimately it is essential that we confront our greatest apprehensions and anxieties and *change the way we think* about everything!

In his book, *The Mind and Brain*, noted psychiatrist, Jeffrey Schwartz, M.D. describes neuroplasticity as:

> *"The ability of neurons to forge new connections, to blaze new paths through the cortex, even to assume new roles. In shorthand, neuroplasticity means rewiring of the brain!"*

He further relates that research in human development shows,

> *"The key finding is that the brain wires itself in response to signals it receives from its environment, a*

Moonlight in Mud Puddles

process very similar to that underlying neuroplasticity in the adult brain, too."

Research also substantiates the amazing truth that a willful, concentrated effort to change one's mindset can actually rewire the neuronal pathways that facilitate consciousness on every level. While certainly not limited to specific disorders, the realization that the anxiety-ridden person is capable of changing their thought processes becomes tremendously empowering.

Change Your Mind!

Change Your Brain!

Change Your Life!

⚬⚬⚬

During an internship for my master's degree in counseling, a young man named Gene was referred to me. He suffered from panic attacks, which actually caused him to faint on at least one occasion, losing consciousness momentarily. Applying newly learned principles of *Systematic Desensitization,* I asked him to describe his thoughts and feelings in a stepwise process leading up to the point of passing out. He shared that he had been walking on the sidewalk when he felt very lightheaded and started to think he was getting sick just before a dull ache began in his chest. He said, "I suddenly found it extremely hard to breathe as the pain got stronger and moved into my throat. My mind was racing, and my heart was pumping hard, and I just knew I was having a heart attack and was going to die right there with no one around to help me! A few minutes later I woke up lying on the sidewalk as the rain came down all around me."

After this episode he said he felt cold and exhausted, but, wasn't as scared anymore, went home to bed, and went right to sleep.

I told Gene that during a panic attack in which I went to the emergency room with similar symptoms, they placed a paper bag over my nose and mouth, telling me to breathe normally until I began to calm down. As the doctor was explaining the breathing process of hyperventilation, I started feeling much better, and after being assured that I wasn't dying, I went home thinking that a paper bag was a whole lot easier than open heart surgery, and determined to try it myself the next time I started feeling that way. I told Gene that I had tried it a couple of times and had not been back to the hospital since.

I suggested that Gene try to hyperventilate on his own at that moment in the office, and if he felt a little anxious, see if a paper bag might work for him too.

He exclaimed, "But I can't make myself have a panic attack. It just happens on its own!"

However, as he began to feel lightheaded, I suggested he tense his chest muscle and see if he could simulate a little of the symptoms to test out the cure.

Within moments, I could see that Gene was experiencing a full-blown panic attack. As he breathed into a small bag that I offered from my pocket, he visibly began to relax and seemed astonished about it all.

I told him that while I hadn't needed to use it for quite a while, I always carried it with me for use, just in case.

During his last session, a few weeks later, Gene reported that he carried the little bag faithfully and had not needed it yet, but felt reassured that he could control it if ever needed.

I knew nothing about neuroplasticity at that time, but it became apparent that both Gene and I were more in control of our thought processes as the panic attacks became almost nonexistent.

———⚜———

Several years later during a post-doctoral internship in San Diego, I worked with a patient exhibiting symptoms of the anxiety disorder known as *agoraphobia,* (abnormal fear of being in public places).

After completing a number of *cognitive-behavioral* sessions in an office setting, I felt that she was ready to attempt a field experiment in the community. After consulting with both she and her husband, and obtaining permission slips signed by each, we got into my car and headed to downtown San Diego in time to arrive at 5 p.m. during rush hour. After parking, we walked together to the corner of 5th Avenue and Broadway and stood together discussing her feelings at the moment.

She said, "It's really loud and intense, but being able to have you here, reassures me that I don't have to be afraid, and I feel okay."

I responded that we should try something "a little different," and after asking her to stay where she was, I walked away from her down an entire city block.

Turning around often to keep an eye on her, I could see that her attention was riveted on watching me walk away, but soon she was distracted, and I was able to duck into a doorway unseen. I then worked my way back to where she was when she wasn't looking, using the crowd and buildings as cover, until I was standing a few feet directly behind her with her back turned away as she anxiously surveyed the chaotic scene.

After a few minutes, I softly called out her name, and she turned back with a shocked expression on her face. "How long have you been standing there?" she exclaimed, "I was terrified without you here!"

I told her that my eyes were constantly on her the entire time and suggested that it was her mind that had betrayed her because I had actually not left her alone.

As we processed her feelings in future sessions, she came to realize that she was safe the whole time whether she realized I was there or not. As a result, she began to understand that the place she needed to feel secure was in her mind, and then she could feel good wherever she was.

She came with her husband for her last session with both of them barely able to contain their enthusiasm. She blurted out, "I did it on my own!"

She recounted that she had gone alone and stood in the same place on the corner of 5th Avenue and Broadway at 5:00 p.m. She related that a couple of times in the first ten minutes she felt a little anxious, but each time she imagined, "I bet he is standing back there and started to relax.

Then she said, "I never actually looked back and thinking I may have left Dr. Ric standing on the corner all alone, I laughed to myself all the way home."

Of course, one trip to confront her anxiety and panic attacks will not be sufficient to bring any cessation to her condition, but it may serve as a reference point to realize the awesome power she has to reframe future incidents into a different outcome. Without question, as we confront our fears courageously and continuously, they diminish significantly, empowering new efforts to gain more self-mastery.

―――――⊱⊰―――――

As previously suggested there are a variety of things which aid the healing process, such as exercise, mindfulness, medication, or even a paper bag. Ultimately, however, getting our "mind right" is essential.

To illustrate this point further, I have often recalled an experience of several years ago, on a bus journey from Twin Falls, Idaho, to Montana for a Christmas vacation. The day before, my wife and I accompanied the house parents from the Moses Lake group home, who were driving further south and leaving us in Twin Falls to catch the bus home the next morning. As we drove into town, we crossed a bridge, suspended hundreds of feet above the Snake river. My anxiety disorder included fear of high bridges, tall buildings, and mountain roads, and I was in panic mode throughout the night in the motel, as I envisioned the morning crossing.

Once we were seated in the bus's front row for extended leg room, I constantly shifted nervously in anticipation of being on the edge, looking down into the chasm. I was suddenly gripped with the urge to relieve my bladder and entered the bathroom at the back of the bus. Standing in the cramped area looking down into the toilet, a thought flashed in my troubled mind, "Wouldn't it be ironic if we were over the abyss at this exact moment," and instead of a debilitating fear, I started laughing at how ludicrous the whole thing was.

I went back to my seat, anxiously awaiting the encounter. After several minutes, I asked my wife if she remembered how far out of town the bridge was, and she replied, "*Oh, we went over that while you were in the bathroom.*"

Immediately, I felt a ridiculous relief, and in subsequent years, when facing similar situations, told myself that I would simply "*Go to the bathroom on the bus!*"

Kedric
How does it help to imagine being in the bus?

Doc
It's just a reminder that all my fears are figments of my imagination, and I can change my mind anytime I choose!

Kedric
Great Idea, but I think it's harder than that, for some things.

Doc

Moonlight in Mud Puddles

Nobody said it would be easy. But the simple things are easier to remember, especially in a moment of crisis. The more you do it, the better it gets.

After many *"**Bathroom Moments,**"* I am now completely free of my fear of bridges. Through it all, I have engaged in my healing journey, and am truly grateful for my times of chaos as I encourage others to believe in themselves, and take more control over their amazing minds.

We are all a Phenomenal Work in Progress!

7
Almost Broken

"It's the children whom the world almost breaks
who grow up to save it."
Raymond Reddington
The Blacklist

Daylight comes as a shock on the streets. Leaving the all-night theatre, I am thrust out into the cold morning air, which overwhelms my senses. On the street, the daytime is much scarier than the night. The light explodes, and I feel unmasked as though everybody knows I'm a phony who at thirteen years old can never be real. I retreat into my alley and wait for the comfort of night to come again.

I have learned to watch the shadows. Hidden from the light, they often reflect the nature and true intent concealed behind the façade. I am highly sensitive to everything around me, as my eyes scan the environment. I try to feel any danger and stay finely tuned to the feelings of fear which burst through my defenses and shake me to the core of my being. The rush demands my attention, as I look for means of escape or defense, if necessary.

I am even more tuned in to the awareness of pleasure. Fear takes precedence, but only for the initial moment, and then I

Moonlight in Mud Puddles

seek to soothe myself. As fear merges into pleasure, sometimes it is hard to tell the difference, and my futile attempt to escape brings more danger than I could ever imagine.

Learning to read people is essential to my survival, and wherever I am or whatever I'm doing, my eyes are never still. I watch people walking by to see if I can make eye contact, or find a sympathetic look, or perhaps, an openness in their vibe and body language. Some of them seem unapproachable, but I try to hone my skills by seeing if I can engage them in conversation and maybe even convince them to support my "cause."

Here comes a well-dressed lady with a smile on her face, but not making eye contact with anyone. Underneath the pleasant exterior, she seems frightened, as though she's worried that in this part of town someone might try to talk to her or rob her jewelry. Instead of looking secure, she appears vulnerable, and the wolves are circling.

Most of the time I just watch and listen. Sometimes I need to close my eyes, shut out the world around me, and pay attention to the impressions of my inner self. Somewhere from deep inside, I can feel the vibrations of the world around me.

Look at the guy walking in front of the rescue mission. He's walking slowly like he doesn't have a care in the world, but something doesn't feel right. His eyes seem to suggest he's a predator, like a panther just waiting to pounce. My inner voice urges caution, and I look as he passes by. I can't quite tell what it is, but something's wrong, and I've learned to trust my intuition. Sometimes it feels like somebody's really cool and safe like the girl just strolling in front of the Brittania. Even from half a block away it feels like she is comfortable in her surroundings. Walking with an easy stride, she looks interesting. I think I'll go talk to her.

Paying attention to my feelings helped, as I made friends, even if they only lasted for a day or two. Together we shared, traded, schemed, and treated each other with a kind of respect because we knew that when it "felt" right, it was better to trust others, showing strength in numbers against a variety of predators. Ultimately, even on the lonely streets, we all just wanted to experience love and acceptance if only for the moment to chase away the blues.

I felt confident that my life experience would be a valuable asset as I started working with troubled kids, but I often felt like an impostor in delivering treatment services. It's difficult to adequately describe being privileged enough to work in the program that I was in as a teenager. Back then my life was in such turmoil that I couldn't imagine ever being successful at anything, let alone having a positive impact upon people like me.

The group homes were staffed by a married couple who lived in a house and attended the needs of up to nine emotionally disturbed teenagers, 24 hours a day for five days. They were both given a full-time salary, a beautiful six-bedroom house in a nice neighborhood, food, gas, and transportation, but by the end of their work week, they needed a well-deserved break from the constant demands of living in such an emotionally draining environment.

Moonlight in Mud Puddles

When I wasn't engaged in fundraising activities, I filled in as a relief houseparent providing two days off for the houseparents, usually working with another staff member. It was there that I came in direct contact with the kids. At first, the opportunity worked well as I shared some of my experiences, but it wasn't long before the street kid inside made his presence known and showed that I had a long way to go as a role model.

The day had seemed uneventful interacting with several of the boys playing catch with a football in the backyard. It was a warm yet pleasant summer's day, and I was enjoying myself as the mood of the whole house was upbeat and positive. Then Wayne, one of the older boys and the dominant Alpha leader in the "pack" began to challenge my authority.

"I don't see why I can't have a pass to go see my girlfriend. Dennis and Shari (the regular house parents) would let me go, and you'll find out if you just call them."

I tried to explain that I was instructed to call them only in an emergency, and his request didn't qualify. With the attention of the others watching closely, Wayne started yelling, "You gotta be the dumbest relief house parent we've ever had. You think you're cool because you were in this program, but that doesn't impress me at all." He continued to taunt. "I bet nobody liked you then either!"

His last remark really got to me because I often felt as though nobody liked me in the past—or the present.

Even though I had already "learned" my lesson about letting others make me mad, somehow at that moment, my enlightenment took flight and left me alone with the dark impulses in my mind. I picked up a nearby piece of wood and had the fleeting impression that all would be well if I just smacked Wayne over the head with it. His response was to taunt me, "Sure big man, bring it on. I'll knock you on your butt in a heartbeat."

Suddenly I realized what I was doing and almost went into shock as I looked at the wood in my hand and the look of satisfaction on Wayne's face.

I dropped the lumber and started to cry. "Maybe you're right that nobody likes me, but I'm starting to like myself, and I just want to apologize for acting so upset."

Like most of the kids in the program, Wayne knew the rage of an abusive parent. What he didn't know was how to react to an adult that was apologizing in tears for being wrong.

"Hey, that's okay man," he exclaimed, "I didn't mean it anyway, and I'm glad you're working with us."

***

Kedric
That would have been a major life lesson. Newsflash: Staff member of Boy's home kills resident. Says he didn't think first.

Doc
That's the point. I caught myself before I exploded.

Kedric
I guess that's a good lesson, which would have been helpful with the "Sweet Roll" caper.

Moonlight in Mud Puddles

Doc

Exactly. Some of the lessons are about how to do it Right, not Wrong, and how to keep it going!

———————————

I have often found that the best way to help troubled kids is to show a vulnerability, which slips in underneath their defenses. At those times a *therapeutic window* opens briefly, and if recognized in time by a caring helper, an opportunity for trust and healing emerges. As we expanded across the state of Washington, I eventually became the "Eastern Division Director" with four group homes under my supervision, including the Soap Lake girls home where I had my office, a girls' home in Colfax, and a boys' home in Ellensburg & Moses Lake.

One day, I was interviewing a tiny and very feisty, independent twelve-year-old girl for acceptance into our new girls home in Soap Lake. The referring caseworker, related that she had been on her own for a year on the streets of Spokane and was very manipulative and difficult to control.

New carpet had just been installed in my office, and as we both sipped on some Kool-Aid, she suddenly held out her glass and menacingly asked, "What would you do if I dumped this grape Kool-Aid all over your new carpet?

I calmly smiled at her, reaching my arm out toward her, and knocked it out of her hand!

Instantly she burst into tears, and with the *therapeutic window* flung wide open, I gently told her that we would love to help her break those destructive patterns, and if she would agree, we would give her a safe, warm home with houseparents who really cared.

She moved in the following weekend and often stopped by to view the purple stain saying, "It reminds me of how crazy I used to be."

To me, it was a reminder of Love.

———⋘✦⋙———

I love the teaching and philosophy of Rudolf Dreikurs who suggested the axiom: *A misbehaving child is a discouraged child.*

The first time I heard this statement, as taught by Dr. Wilma Perry of Warner Pacific College, I thought to myself, "Wow! Somebody gets it."

I was stunned, yet excited. Such an amazing, self-evident truth was being proclaimed by a dynamic college professor who seemed to understand that all human beings misbehave because they feel bad about themselves. I was enraptured with this revelation, which seemed like *illuminated enlightenment from the top of the mountain.*

Suddenly, I could not only relate, but felt that if I could be assigned a life task, I would want to take the message to as many troubled kids (no matter what age) as possible.

To actually understand the message is to change our entire outlook and response when we see misbehavior because instead of rebellion, we see discouragement. Instead of feeling their anger, we feel their pain. Instead of the problem child we see ourselves, for we have all felt the weight of discouragement and even misbehavior.

During my years of being a runaway, survival required that I rarely allowed my feelings of loneliness, discouragement, and defeat to rise to consciousness. The truth is that because I felt that way *all* of the time, I could never be open or vulnerable about that with anybody, especially myself!

For me having a parent, teacher, counselor, or any caregiver, "get it" would and did open the door to the potential of truth, bonding, and healing.

Dr. Dreikurs taught that rather than giving in to the dysfunctional demands of an angry child, we should identify their mistaken goals of misbehavior and respond with more appropriate interventions.

"Never Give Attention on Demand"

"Bow out of Power Struggles"

"Do the Unexpected"

Adopting these techniques was really helpful with kids who were manipulative.

In all of our group homes, we instituted a behavior modification system designed to motivate needed changes in the resident's behavior. One of the older boys, named Dale, was doing well on the system with exemplary behavior for several weeks in a row. As a treatment team, the house parents, school teachers, and I met to discuss Dale's future and had all agreed that he was ready to go back to his parents' home in Western Washington.

The Sunday before Dale's release, the group home

staff took the boys to the Moses Lake Presbyterian church, as was their custom. Dale had been selected as an usher to help take up the collection plate for several past Sundays because of his trustworthiness and also in an attempt to reward him for displaying such responsible behavior.

After the service, which I also attended, the house parents approached me and said "We can't find Dale. You don't think he would run away just a few days before he goes home for good, do you?"

I was bewildered because no reasonable explanation made any sense for the situation as presented. At that moment the pastor and the head usher appeared and said, "The morning offering is missing, and the last person to see it was Dale. Could we please talk to him?"

With a feeling of impending doom, I explained to them, that Dale was also missing, and we suspected he had run away.

"But why would he do that?" the pastor exclaimed, "We trusted him!"

The truth is that there is no logical answer for the self–destructive and self-defeating action that Dale brought upon himself other than the reality staring us in the face. Like so many other troubled persons, Dale was far more comfortable with failure than success.

As long as the structure of the program was in place to motivate his behavioral change, Dale was able to perform to the best of his considerable potential; however, his own self-image did not allow embracing the visage of a successful young adult, and faced with the prospect of being on his own, maintaining responsible behavior was more than he could handle.

As I look back on my misguided attempts to produce more failure than success, I am reminded that people don't make good choices until they feel good about themselves. It is a lifelong process.

With Dale, who I never heard from again, the seeds of hope had been planted.

While working with emotionally disturbed teenagers was often very rewarding, There were incidents, like Dale, that were excruciatingly painful and disheartening when we had to admit failure, and give up on kids that we often loved and cared for the most. Mark was another one of those kids.

When I first met him, he was being held at the Pierce County Juvenile Detention Center in Tacoma, Washington. As he was escorted into the room for the intake interview to be considered for placement in one of our group homes, I was struck with his demure appearance. He was quite small for a teenager of fourteen years and sat with his knees drawn up and his head down. His arms encircled his legs, squeezing them tightly.

The male detention staff warned, "Don't let his appearance fool you. He can be a demon, and if you need any help, I'll be right outside this door." I assured him that I felt capable of handling the situation and thanked him for his concern.

Mark raised his head, and looked at me with huge

dark eyes, and with a puppy dog look on his face declared, "I don't know what he's talking about, I'm actually very nice, and if you let me come to the group home, I promise I won't cause any trouble."

After the interview, while I was not oblivious to his manipulation, I sincerely felt we could help him, and offered a placement in the home in Moses Lake.

When Mark arrived, he was quiet and withdrawn as if he spent most of his time in a far away world inside his head, which of course, I understood. We gave him time to adjust to his new environment as the newest of nine boys, (with several older than he) and being the smallest, he was picked on and ordered around by the older kids, but he remained quiet and seemed to ignore them. The only exception was when he wanted something from one of the adults. Then Mark was absolutely charming. He had a full head of silky black hair, porcelain-like features, and large black/brown eyes that gave the appearance of innocence and warmth.

He was obviously used to manipulating adults with his size and looks, especially when they were looking for some kind of cooperation from a troubled kid. Of course, neither the houseparents or residents of the group home were greatly moved by this performance, and it wasn't long before we witnessed what the detention staff were referring to in the first interview.

I received a call at home from the houseparent, on a calm Saturday afternoon. "Ric, I can't hold on to him, and he's completely out of control. What should I do?

I said, "Who? What are you talking about?"

Moonlight in Mud Puddles

The houseparent, who was later to become a Montana Highway Patrolman and was very capable and controlled, responded, "It's Mark. He's in a complete freak-out episode, and I can't stop him or get him calmed down."

I reassured him that I would be there in twenty minutes, and we would handle it together. When I arrived, I could hear Mark screaming from an upstairs bedroom. As I joined the houseparent in the room, I tried to remain calm as I told Mark that he would have to control himself or we would have to restrain him so he wouldn't hurt himself or anyone else. He glared at me and taunted me saying, "just try it, big man, I'm not afraid of you." And with that, he squirted past me and took off running downstairs and throughout all the house.

I finally caught him from behind as he started back up the stairs, and holding on as tight as I could, Mark struggled to get free for at least fifteen minutes as we lay in the middle of the stairs. Finally, I could feel him start to release the tension as he allowed his head to sink into my chest, crying softly and whimpering with each ragged breath.

Instinctively, and also being exhausted, I lay there holding him tightly, gently whispering that everything was going to be okay.

We stayed in that position, with an incredible feeling of bonding for an additional fifteen minutes. Lying with Mark on the stairs was a powerful healing experience in part because, like many emotionally disturbed children, he had been physically, and perhaps sexually, abused as a child. As a result, simply being touched in an embrace can be especially frightening because on a subconscious level, enduring a hug feels like giving up control to a potential abuser, and the "fight or flight" response is automatic within the developing brain.

Research in attachment and bonding has shown that in the midst of being restrained in the devoted arms of a caregiver, a healing transition occurs when the child finally submits, and the new sensory experience stimulates positive associations. Subconsciously with Mark, it was like being soothed by a loving parent, and we both felt it.

Mark stayed in the group home for several months, and each time he saw me, there was a deep connection between us that we both felt. There were occasional outbursts but he was able to gain control before things escalated, and it seemed he might become another of our success stories.

It was a sinking feeling when I got the call at 3 a.m. saying that Mark had a knife and was threatening to cut another boy unless we immediately removed him from the home and asked a judge to place him in the state school at Echo Glen, to be with his older brother. When I got to the home at 3:30 a.m., I told Mark that I would do everything in my power to suggest a judge follow his request, and we placed him quietly in the back seat of the group home van.

During the thirty-minute ride to the detention center in Ephrata, I commented to the houseparent, making certain that Mark overheard me.

"This is the reason we do the work we do, because this

Moonlight in Mud Puddles

is a young man that's worth everything we can offer, and even though it looks like we have failed with him tonight, someday he will remember that we really loved him and always will, and hopefully turn his life into something that will make us proud."

It's tough to lose a child like that, but I believe in the power of love and still believe that his future is bright.

8

Grandma's Recipe

"Or perhaps people were like recipes, he pondered now, and the key to success was in finding the ingredients you had to remove, the components that turned all the others bitter, excessively salty, difficult to swallow, even too jarringly sweet."
Julia Glass
The Whole World Over

One of the hardest things to accept as a family therapist is not knowing what happened to patients after therapy is finished. Of course, as trained professionals, we are encouraged to maintain objectivity without emotional involvement. However, therapeutic skills require an emotional investment, and I often wonder about the lives that have been impacted by our time together.

I have often thought about Mark and Dale, as evidenced by their inclusion in this writing, because the circumstances of their departures were both so sudden, allowing no closure of any kind. Had Dale simply gone home as scheduled, I would have remembered him as a success story, showing the effectiveness of our group home program. Instead, his actions indicated that we had failed to recognize a much deeper issue that had not even surfaced through any aspect of our treatment services. In addition to the impression that he was more comfortable with failure than success, it is also possible that Dale couldn't face going back into the family system from which he emanated.

As a treatment team, we knew very little of Dale's family of origin. I remember that his father was a highly successful professional like a medical doctor, lawyer, or perhaps a judge. Was it conceivable that Dale was viewed by his parents as a blight upon their reputation and standing in the community? In hindsight, it seems not only conceivable but likely. Like myself as a runaway on the streets, Dale may have simply been afraid of going home.

I knew a little more about Mark's family because a probation officer at the detention center had written a psychosocial history. His father was a merchant marine who was at sea for weeks at a time, as he traveled all over the world. His mother was quite passive and wanted to counterbalance the father's autocratic parenting style. As a result, her two boys were given free rein when the father wasn't home, but when he was, they were expected to toe the line, with abusive punishment following any perceived infraction of the rules.

This ambiguity allowed Mark and his older brother—by two years—to avoid being home as much as possible, and as they grew into teenagers, trouble with the law seemed inevitable.

As opposed to Dale who may have been afraid to go

home, Mark most likely felt that his real home was wherever his brother was, and on the night that precipitated his departure, that is all he said he wanted. He wanted to be with his family, and who could blame him?

———⟣⟣⟣⟣⟣———

Back in the 1970s, working in our group home program, I knew nothing about the fledgling family-therapy movement in psychology. When I applied for entrance into a doctoral program in the field, I was under the impression that family therapy simply meant getting all the family members together in one room for counseling. Of course, that can be an objective for a well-trained family therapist, but it is also possible to do the work with an individual alone, because of the influence of generations of family members which are implanted within as a result of the family system.

Beyond the scope of the genetic predetermination, the family system instills in its members' patterns of behavior and attitudes, which impact every emotional and social involvement in an individual's life. Families tend to maintain internal stability and resist change, in a process called "homeostasis." Maintaining the homeostatic balance can be healthy if members are encouraged to be open with each other and able to move toward independence and personal growth. However, in a family which encourages secrecy and unreasonable loyalties, personal growth is stunted, and the homeostasis becomes dysfunctional, keeping individual members locked in a pattern of allegiance to the family hierarchy and the needs

Moonlight in Mud Puddles

as defined by the system.

When one member seeks to move beyond the expectations of the family as a whole, the others attempt to discourage, or even disparage, the individual effort to bring them back into the fold.

"Since the old country, we have always been plumbers. If you pursue this misguided quest to become an artist, you will break your father's heart because you know he wants all of his children to follow in his footsteps into the family business. But, I guess you might as well, because you don't really love him anyway!"

Many family members have given up their dreams and talents because of the stifling impact of a dysfunctional family system. This is often true in marital dysfunction, where a spouse is unable to confront their own issues and requires their partner to remain dysfunctional in order to "help" them, instead of pursuing goals that could help them both get healthy.

In my early years as a therapist, a woman in her late forties named Helen came to see me about John, her husband of 24 years. She stated that John's alcoholism was driving her crazy, and she was thinking about divorce. In order to help her become self-empowered to make choices in her own best interest, I asked her to write a "little life history" about her life before she married John. At first, she protested that she wanted to help with John's problems and she didn't see how looking at her life could help. I further encouraged her to let me glimpse a little of the conditions surrounding her choices to marry an alcoholic in the first place, hoping that she could break any patterns to help her make better choices in the future.

She agreed to put something in writing. She arrived for the next session with a hand-written note on one page of a tablet-sized paper.

I read the lines which said, "At the age of four, I witnessed my father blow my mother's head off with a shotgun in the backyard. The police came and separated me from my siblings, placing us in different homes. I went to my grandfather's house. He started sexually molesting me around age eight or nine, and I met and married John when I was sixteen (he was twenty-four) in order to get out of the house."

After reading the note, I suggested that there may be a few issues which could have impacted her life! She replied, "But that's all past stuff, and I just need to know how to deal with John."

I asked if she thought John might come to a session or two of his own, and she replied, "I will make sure he does."

When John came to his session, I was surprised to learn that he had quit drinking eight years earlier, to please his wife. He stated, "Everything I try to do for her doesn't seem to help. She is always angry at something—mostly me."

In the next session with Helen, I asked her about John's drinking, and she replied, "He is still an alcoholic, he just isn't drinking." I was familiar with the concept of a "dry drunk" who still has the underlying issues, but

103

Moonlight in Mud Puddles

John seemed willing to work on his own stuff.

She started missing her scheduled weekly appointments, but John attended his sessions faithfully. After a few sessions, he told me that Helen wanted him to stop seeing me because, "He wasn't getting any better, and I certainly wasn't helping her!"

Helen's victimization was so severe that she was unable to face any of her own issues. She needed John to stay "sick" in order to help him, maintaining the only identity she knew; the only sense of personal value she possessed.

Dr. van der Kolk says,

"If you grew up unwanted and ignored, it is a major challenge to develop a visceral sense of agency and self-worth."

Helen's entire life existed inside someone else's world, because she couldn't face her own.

In the book, *Do I Have to Give Up ME to be Loved By YOU,* the authors quote Clint Weyand as saying,

"My love must be willing to let you grow in directions I haven't traveled. If I don't give you this freedom, my love is only a thinly disguised method for controlling you."

The homeostatic balance is powerful and influences many decisions within the family system. This influence is a dynamic flow which contributes to either a successful function in its participants or to that of a dysfunctional failure. More often, families facilitate a synthesis of both; thus the choice of the individual member is to embrace the ascendancy or break the pattern of defeat.

Depending on the level of dysfunction experienced by the parents and embraced and passed down from when they were children, their own family maintains its structure and balance as each member functions in a subconscious and unwritten role according to the needs of the family as a whole. Although given various names by different theorists, each role is similar in its form and service to the family dynamic. The parents often fit into several possibilities such as:

- *The Enforcer*—who supervises the actual and implied rules such as, "no one leaves the dinner table until everyone is finished" or "children don't speak unless spoken to first by an adult."

- *The Enabler*—who, afraid of confrontation or discord, allows others to continue in misbehavior or addiction, for fear of reprisal.

- *The Martyr*—who functions as a victim in agony over the attitudes and behavior of other members who wound them deeply, and who usually announce it with very pointed guilt trips. "That's OK son, go out and have a good time—I'll just sit here alone in the dark."

- *The Co-dependent*—who serves the sickness of the addict by offering to facilitate provisions of the substance as desired. The spouse of a food addict says, "May I pick up this 8 lb. banana cream pie for you on my way home? It's on sale, and I know you'll love it."

105

The children also provide service in roles designed to take attention off the family dysfunction:

- *The Hero* (or Golden Child)—who is the perfect angel as evidenced by being an overachiever, respectful, responsible, and successful in everything they do. "Look at my son, he's the quarterback and homecoming king, as well as valedictorian, with a 4.0 grade point average. We are so proud of him."

- *The Scapegoat* or *(Identified Patient)*—who in contrast to the Hero (often an older sibling) is a disruptive devil, a rule-breaker, in trouble most of the time, with poor grades, requiring and draining the attention and energy of the rest of the family. "She just won't listen and is so rebellious, that her only friends are a bad influence on everybody. I just wish you could be more like your older brother—we had no problems raising him."

- *The Parentified Child*—They assume the position within the family as caretaker of the younger children when mother has a headache or father is incapacitated by illness or addiction. Their mannerisms and speech are erudite, indicative of "wisdom" beyond their years. Often functioning as a surrogate partner to one of the parents, if the other is missing or incapable.

Of course these "roles" are not as clearly defined as presented, and often overlap as the family dynamics change and expand or contract, but unless the chain is broken, they are subconsciously embraced and passed down to succeeding generations.

Breaking the dysfunctional patterns of our own family system is frightening. Our entire mind-set, world-view, and belief system is tied to the ground from which we have sprung and uprooting some of that which is deeply planted is to destroy so much of what we have cultivated. Everything that we are as domesticated humans lies rooted in someone else's belief system based on their country of origin, society, race, religion, and a host of dynamics beyond our personal control or choice.

As Ruiz relates in *The Four Agreements*,

"That is why we need a great deal of courage to challenge our own beliefs. Because even if we know we didn't choose all these beliefs it is also true that we agreed (conformed) to all of them. The agreement is so strong that even if we understand the concept of it not being true, we feel the blame, the guilt, and the shame that occur if we go against the rules."

I heard a noted family therapist speak at a conference for "Adult Children of Dysfunctional Families" relate that he was involved in a number of failed business enterprises with his alcoholic father, until he decided to go into a business that his father wanted no part of and became an alcohol counselor!

We all have to take the risk of disapproval and even disinheritance, to have the courage to challenge the family system, and that is made even more difficult depending on the role we have within our family of origin.

After my parents divorced, and my mother remarried the abusive stepfather, I became the *scapegoat* in my family, and although the role began in early adolescence, it was perpetuated into adulthood. Once I was "typecast," it was difficult to be viewed as any other image by others or myself. Since I adapted quickly to play the role and embraced it wholeheartedly, it was soon ingrained into my psyche and self-concept.

Even though I have worked hard to change my internal thought processes, it is still distressing to abandon the belief that the *scapegoat* is a part of my true self.

Kedric
Maybe that's why you seem like a troublemaker. You believe that's your identity.

Doc
Troublemaker or Teacher, it's all the same. The main thing we are looking for is the *Power to Change*.

Kedric
Excellent. I really like being kind and generous and not in trouble all the time.

Doc
Feels good, doesn't it?

To illustrate the process and the change needed to break with the erroneous beliefs and dysfunctional patterns of the family system, I offer the following depiction of a celebrated event in the household of my mother's third husband (who, for clarification, is not the abusive step-father of my early adolescence).

This vignette is predicated upon the axiom: ***What You Don't Pass Back...You Pass On!***

At a family Thanksgiving Dinner in the thirty-five-foot-long living room, the tables were placed end to end and covered with table cloths to give the appearance of one dining room table almost twenty feet long. The elegant china with a rose pattern and the silverware handed down from past generations adorned the place settings. Crystal goblets and embroidered cloth napkins held in place by ceramic holders supplied the finishing touch. The serving dishes and plates were part of the rose-patterned china set, except for the main delicacy which would be served on an exquisite platter of etched silver.

Seating was arranged with place cards positioned in the tails of little ceramic turkeys with the names of each family member and guest handwritten on each card. It was understood that one's place at the table was designed on a grander scheme to facilitate conversation and deportment of the children and was not negotiable.

At one end sat my step-father, The Honorable Francis Bardanouve, Elder Statesman in the Montana State Legislature who served with distinction for thirty-six years without interruption. At the other end by the buffet table upon which the delicious fare was to be served, sat the matriarch of the family, Dr. Venus Bardanouve, no less distinguished than her husband, in

Moonlight in Mud Puddles

her own field of Audiology and Speech and Hearing Therapy.

She was also my incredible mother.

As each dish was served, Mother handed them first to me, seated next to her on the left, and then after taking a healthy portion, I passed it down to my daughter, Amanda who was sitting next to her three brothers, Clint, Eric, and Brian. The well prepared, succulent delicacies were passed around the table to each family member and guest until the last person in line placed each behind my mother, to sit once again upon the serving table.

As the green beans with bacon, cranberries, mashed potatoes with gravy, and other cuisines, were handed down from my mother, it was a privilege to offer each to my own children who, in future years, would repeat this wonderful family ritual to children of their own.

Then, with great flourish, the main dish was about to be presented as mother reminded us all that it was a special preparation from a family recipe passed down from succeeding generations over hundreds of years, and it was a family tradition of which we were all privileged to partake. Finally, there it was. The sustenance, consisting of a host of generational dysfunction that had fed, fascinated, and bewildered so many ancestors.

A silver platter overflowing with:

Family Shit!

Mother, turning toward me with the silver platter in hand, smiled ingratiatingly and said, "Ric, would you like some of our life-sustaining family Recipe?" (because she would never say 'Shit')

I, of course, took a generous helping as I have always done, and then turned toward my five-year-old daughter who was seated next to me so I could serve her and held out the beautiful silver platter.

Suddenly, as I looked into her trusting and expectant eyes, I realized that I just couldn't pass it on anymore.

Hesitating, I thought that I had no right to interrupt this family tradition for the others like my sister, Libby, with her own children, also seated around the table. However, reeling from my sudden epiphany, I knew that I had to pass it back to my well-meaning mother, whom I sincerely believed wanted only the best for her family.

"Mom, I have enough of my own problems, and needing to work on them myself as an independent adult, I must pass back anything that's not good for me, regardless of what anyone believes is right for me."

To Pass It Back does not mean that we go to family members and attempt to change their attitudes, or beliefs, parenting style, addictions, or anything else that we perceive is dysfunctional. As Adult Children of Dysfunctional Families, healing does not include confronting an addicted parent and demanding change, threatening isolation from loved ones, or some other punishment to whip them into shape.

What it does mean, however, is that if your parents' religious belief system (for example) is too rigid or not in harmony with your own thinking or experience, rather than demanding that your own children profess the generational faith, you break from the pattern and follow your own path.

What You Don't Pass Back…You Pass On!

In my family there is much of value that I wish to pass on to my loved ones, including wonderful traditions

Moonlight in Mud Puddles

such as our Family Thanksgiving Dinner after which we played board games, had a scavenger hunt, talked and laughed together, with a magical bonding that I will always love.

One of my favorite definitions of the functional vs. the dysfunctional family is that both are full of problems, conflicts, addictions, strengths, and weaknesses, but the functional family attempts to confront them openly and honestly, communicating with each other without guilt or reprisal, encouraging every member to engage willingly in the change process.

The dysfunctional family does exactly the opposite. But every family has dysfunctional patterns, which need to be identified and relinquished in order to become healthy. Breaking the patterns of dysfunction within the family system can certainly be frightening, depending on the amount of resistance encountered by each member. But the resulting change can also be liberating as members are taught to think for themselves, learn to own their areas of frailty and fault, and see every failure as an opportunity of transformation, providing new ingredients to pass on to all generations.

9
Into the Unknown

"When you walk to the edge of all the light you have and take that first step into the darkness of the unknown you must believe that one of two things will happen. There will be something solid for you to stand upon or you will be taught to fly."
Patrick Overton
The Leaning Tree

When I recite some of the experiences of my life to students or persons who do not know me well, I have often heard them exclaim incredulously, "are you making all of this up, or perhaps just exaggerating a little?" As a result, it becomes a difficult task to explain that having been a teenage runaway who lived the lie that I was really an adult, with stories that were made up to procure funds or find companionship, I actually abhor deceit, and often am engaged in a brutal honesty without apparent regard of consequence to myself or others.

Following a suspicious probe of my truthfulness from a graduate student after reading *Wisdom from the Streets,* I implored my mother, whose reputation is impeccable, to pen a succinct statement concerning the veracity of my writing. In response, she wrote that "the events as described actually happened, and I know them as truthful because I also lived through them myself." She also told me that in addition to whatever she was reading, she perused my book daily, and always found "something of value" that she enjoyed.

Notwithstanding the truth as presented, however, no statement has ever induced more skepticism than my proclamation that I have been an ordained minister in the denomination named, "The Assemblies of God" pastored in Alaska and California, and even preached (briefly) on television.

Becoming an ordained minister was prompted by the idea that as I traveled representing Youth Outreach, Inc. in various churches and service clubs to raise funds and awareness of our work with troubled kids, it may produce a legitimacy not otherwise available.

Having been credentialed as such did help to provide access to a wider variety of supporters and organizations, even though the reputation of Vancouver Boys Academy/Youth Outreach, Inc. was inimitable on its own. I also had access to other agencies working with delinquent youth that were approved by the denomination. In this way, I became aware of the "Alaskan Youth Village" in Juneau, whose executive director was also an ordained minister with the Assemblies of God.

After 8 ½ years representing Youth Outreach, Inc., it became evident that being gone from home so often, placed too much strain on my marriage and family, which now included our firstborn son, Clint, who was just a year old. I subsequently resigned to accept a position with the "Alaskan Youth Village" and moved to Juneau for another new beginning full of promise, which was yet another disaster just waiting for my arrival.

The clash of personalities between myself and the executive director rivaled that of David and Goliath, and without further ado, I was fired after six months. The Presbyter for Assemblies of Southeast Alaska suggested that he would recommend me as pastor for a little church of about 40 people in Haines, but I would have to "try out" by preaching a sermon, after which the members would vote to retain or send me down the road. Of course, while I knew nothing about the administration of a church, I was more confident in my speaking ability, having represented the organization often during most of the previous decade.

After a rousing message of which I remember nothing, I was voted in by a count of 39 to 1. I often wondered who the misfit was (other than the obvious) and was surprised a year later when my right-hand man told me that he always resisted going along with the crowd, and thus voted against my acceptance. In hindsight, it became apparent why I selected him to assist me, being like-minded in so many ways.

I loved Alaska. I quickly learned some of what it meant to identify myself with being a rugged, independent, free thinker who had left the lower 48 to make his way in the Last Frontier. I was often surprised for instance when someone pointed out an individual who had been a corporate lawyer in New York and had dropped out of the rat race to become a cook in a local café. Many such persons from different walks of life became part of the society of Alaskans. It reminded me of John Galt, the secret inventor of the revolutionary motor in the book *Atlas Shrugged* who would not allow his invention to be squandered by a greed-filled society, and left the world behind to seek true fulfillment. I soon felt that, as an Alaskan, I could be a paragon in one of Ayn Rand's novels, as I ventured out to impact the community of believers in that magical setting.

I also soon learned that my new image was not embraced by many who were native to the state or at least had lived there for a very long time. They referred to me as a "Cheechako," which I discovered was the equivalent of a "Dude" or "Dandy," dressed up in silk clothes pretending to be a working cowboy on a Montana ranch.

Whether Cheechako or Sourdough, I loved being in Alaska and that was enough for me, whatever I was called.

People also started calling me "Pastor," and that did not fit my self-image, so I suggested they refer to me as plain old "Ric." I was gently rebuked by a wise parishioner named Helen who informed me that people needed to use the term out of respect for the position as someone who was their spiritual leader, and suggested I refer to myself that way, for their sake.

I acquiesced but wasn't sure I could ever see myself as "spiritual."

For the first few months, being the pastor in a growing church was exciting. I gave sermons at least three times a week, officiated at a wedding, a funeral, led singing and worship, and began to institute new ways of reaching out to touch hearts and meet needs in the community beyond the members of the congregation. We started a coffee house ministry in a house next to the church building to help travelers who came through the town on their way north to the Yukon and the mainland of Alaska. People throughout the area started to take notice of all the activity, and attendance started rising.

It seemed that I had finally found my true calling and began to feel that I would stay for the remainder of my days at the Haines Christian Center in Alaska, the land many called "God's Country."

It wasn't long, however, before I began to be aware of ripples of discontent among some of the more established members of the congregation. As they gathered together in homes following the Sunday morning service, I soon realized the main nourishment was a dish aptly called "Roast Pastor." It fueled the energy of those who were hungry for a transfiguration back to "the way we always had church, before this Cheechako introduced all the changes that don't fit with who we are."

Without realizing it at the time, the Street Kid inside dealt with the criticisms by wanting to run, believing they were right about my being a misfit who would never conform to the image everyone seemed to want.

Fortunately, there were others like Teresa, (the music director) and Jim and Edna (who started a tape ministry of my sermons) that were life-sustaining, and I resolved to stay the course and make the best of it.

Having earned my master's degree in counseling from the University of Portland while working at Youth Outreach, Inc., I began to offer counseling services to not only members of the congregation, but to those of the Haines community as well. It was in this context that an event occurred that was to change my thinking, and indeed the course of my entire life.

----------·⟨⟨⟨⟩⟩⟩·----------

Following a Christmas pageant, in which Teresa recruited and directed a small orchestra to complement the choir, she mentioned to me that the French-horn player wanted to talk to me, but was shy and reclusive and didn't know how to approach me. She related further that he had been a musician with a well-known orchestra on the East Coast, but had become disillusioned, and now lived with his wife and grown daughter in a backwoods cabin thirty miles out of town.

In bringing him to me, we all sat down together, and Teresa said, "it's about his daughter, and I told him that you are a counselor who may be able to help." The father, a small gray-haired man in his early sixties, remained quiet, but nodded as Teresa continued, "She is running barefoot through the forest near the cabin, tearing off her clothes and screaming at the top of her lungs as though someone is chasing her."

I told the father that Teresa and I would come soon with a couple of his friends from our congregation to see if we could help if he wanted us to do so. He responded, "please come as soon as possible."

The next day, Teresa and I were joined by Ida and Helen who were acquainted with the family, as we rode in the church's four-wheel drive vehicle because the road to the cabin was almost inaccessible. When we reached the cabin, both father and mother greeted us saying, "we told her you were coming, and when she heard you on the road, she stripped off her robe and ran naked into the woods!"

After Helen grabbed a blanket to wrap her in, we started searching for her and found her sitting at the base of a tree about 50 yards from the cabin. Looking at us with eyes that appeared terrified she screamed, repeatedly, "What do you want? What do you want?"

Wrapping her in the blanket, the women stroked her hair and back, while soothingly telling her that I was the pastor of the church, and we just wanted to help her not be so afraid when she was alone. We quickly realized that she was in no state of mind to talk to us about what was troubling her, and I told her we only wanted to pray for her, promising that God loved her and wanted her to be set free from the chains that seemed to bind her.

Upon returning to the church building where the cars were parked, Helen stayed behind in the truck for a moment to ask me a question.

"Pastor, you preach such powerful sermons about God wanting to set people free from pain and sickness... but when we prayed for her today nothing happened! *Why doesn't it work?*"

Moonlight in Mud Puddles

I turned toward Helen and honestly said, "I don't know what to pray about… because *I don't know what's wrong with her!*"

This harrowing experience soon became the most prominent and incessant thought in my mind, as I repeatedly heard Helen's accusation, "but, *why doesn't it work?*" I began to search for answers, but without access to a professional library (ten years before the Internet), I realized that while I had a Master of Counseling degree, I knew very little about treating mental illness.

Being a pastor was somewhat fulfilling, but excitement seemed to build as I perused the idea of seeking further education to satisfy my quest.

I started emphasizing my counseling outreach, in addition to preaching, but neglected other pastoral duties, like visitation to members who often felt neglected and needed a shepherd who paid close attention to the needs of the flock.

I began looking at doctoral programs in a reference book on universities at the local library and found a program in Family Therapy that looked interesting. I reasoned with myself that, instead of applying to several schools, I would apply to just one, and if accepted, I would pursue it as my destiny.

Within a few months, I was accepted for the fall session into the doctoral program at United States International University (now Alliant International) in San Diego, California and had been approved for a low-interest education loan from the State of Alaska with payments deferred until after graduation. By May 1, everything was prepared and ready for our departure on the 15th of July.

The church was receptive and supportive, and the next two and half months were filled with many invitations to dinner and coffee time, as we said our good-byes. In just two years, the church membership was over a hundred, the building had a new addition, we were actively engaged in the coffeehouse, and outreach to the community with a variety of activities which brought people together to share the excitement and blessings we were experiencing as a congregation.

———◦◦◦———

One profound encounter helped to confirm that my decision to move in a new direction was well advised. It had been Jim and his wife, Edna, who had started a tape ministry by recording my sermons and teachings, sending them by mail to members and others by request, and now Jim invited me for a drive so we could speak in private. Jim was an old fisherman who was one of the most honest and direct people I have ever known. I had appointed him to be the adult Sunday School Teacher, and on several occasions, as he was getting enthusiastic and worked up exhorting class members, he would punctuate his teaching with swear words of encouragement. "Dammit, people, we just have to batten down the hatches and push through the storm!"

Any time Jim had something to say, he didn't mince words. He told it as he saw it, but with an underlying gentleness and love that made the message as good as gold. Sitting in the truck parked alongside the road, Jim said, "Pastor, I'm just going to tell you something that I feel really strong about. When you go to California for school, see if you can get a job working with people in trouble, or as an evangelist preaching in different churches, but don't try to get a job leading a church, because..." (at this point Jim looked at me with tears in his eyes)... *"You are the best preacher I have ever heard... and the worst pastor!"*

Kedric
Perhaps a street hustler doth not a good pastor make.

Doc
Instead, perhaps it is good to know your limitations so you can concentrate on your strengths.

Jim's edict was strong but had such a ring of truth in it that I trusted it immediately. Many people in the church would view their pastor as a beloved leader who must be capable of servanthood in such a wide variety of functions, and I knew that I just didn't measure up. I responded to Jim with a hug and told him that I loved and respected him more than he could ever imagine!

On July 15, we left Haines, Alaska, as scheduled, pulling a homemade trailer behind our station wagon, as we ferried to Prince Rupert, British Columbia, where we would begin our drive all the way to San Diego!

I love road trips usually, but with our one-year-old son Eric, sitting in his car seat next to his mother, screaming and crying most of the trip, we all were ecstatic when we arrived five days later. In addition to Eric, our 3 ½-year-old son, Clint, offered his own unique style to make the trip more interesting. In Haines, Clint had learned to wave to all oncoming cars and say "Hi!" to everyone he encountered because it was a small town courtesy and camaraderie that was shared by most. As a result, Clint smiled and waved to everybody which was reasonable, but saying "Hi!" to everyone in restaurants and wherever we stopped, became an almost tragic lesson in social mores and customs, in decidedly different cultures.

Being rejected frequently with looks of disdain, with only occasional returned greetings, Clint's feelings were being trounced upon. I took Clint aside after one particular scathing encounter, and hugging him, said, "People here are just really busy paying attention to a lot of things, so I suggest you just smile and wait for them to wave or say "hi" before you do." Clint seemed to accept that, often repeating to me, "they're just really busy, huh, Dad," as he adapted to the new social norm.

Although, I'm not sure he ever really abandoned his upbringing, because, even as an adult, Clint is one of the friendliest and most personable guys you could ever meet!

The "Street Kid" unwittingly exerted influence as I

Moonlight in Mud Puddles

looked for employment situations which would accommodate being a full-time doctoral student, attending
classes evenings and weekends, for, in spite of knowing
that Jim was right, my survival mode kicked in, and I
looked for pastoral positions anyway.

Soon, I became the Pastor of the Poway Christian
Center in North San Diego County where I stayed for
Three and a half years until I received my Ph.D. in Psy-
chology.

The church at first, responded much like the one in
Haines, with an increase in membership, a building ex-
pansion, my counseling ministry, and about half of the
established members upset because I didn't meet their
expectations. At the end of that experience, I saw that
Jim was a sage with esoteric wisdom, and I knew I must
never attempt to pastor another church, no matter how
well I was received initially or how desperate I got.

I was a former "Street Kid," still rebelling against the
establishment, who was better at helping others with issues similar to mine. I needed to emphasize what I was
good at rather than trying to live up to the expectations
of others who saw my potential, but became furious with
my performance. I also had a lot of lessons yet to learn,
as I continued matriculation in the Graduate School of
Good Intentions, marked with self-destruction and chaos just around every corner.

10
Soul Train

"There is nothing more important to true growth
than realizing that you are not the voice of the mind
- you are the one who hears it."
Michael A. Singer
The Untethered Soul - The Journey Beyond Yourself

Driven by the desire to be able to identify and effectively treat the condition in which I encountered the girl in the woods, I became fascinated by the study of the psyche.

Translated from the Greek as **Soul**, the psyche includes the mind., the will, and the emotions. Thus my quest crystallized into an investigation of the mind and brain, the spectrum of mental health and illness, and the physical and spiritual pathways of emotion. The question of how the mechanics of a physical brain can generate awareness of trauma so severe that it is capable of protecting itself by a process such as dissociation seems nothing short of the miraculous to me.

Most persons simply take for granted a reality in which human beings are able to think and feel with a perceptual awareness, subjectively experiencing a host of emotions to fit any situation which may be encountered.

But that reality is distorted when circumstances are presented such as watching myself being assaulted across the room and feeling amazed to think that *I have a brain that is capable of protecting me when I'm not able to protect myself.*

No explanation is sufficient which suggests that it was simply my imagination. Somehow, the puzzle pieces do not fit merely by the idea that our brains are wired to accommodate such a dilemma.

Even with our limited knowledge, we are aware that we cannot place thousands of integrated circuits into a container expecting them to find their way into connections capable of producing a device to access the Internet. Just having the circuitry doesn't create a computer, any more than having three pounds of meat inside the skull produces a conscious awareness of everything we know.

I find studies of psychophysiology intriguing as neuroscience explores areas of the brain, which correlate as an example, to the function of various emotions or our perceptions of the way others feel. However, to have knowledge of the way it works is still not the same as knowing that it does. Dr. Jeffrey Schwartz, in his book, *The Mind and the Brain,* illuminates the limitation,

> *"that there is a very real difference between understanding the physiological mechanisms of perception and having a conscious perceptual experience."*

To illustrate the absurdity of the rise of consciousness within the physical brain Dr. Schwartz tells the story of a conversation between an alien commander and a scout who has just returned from Earth to report the results of his reconnaissance:

"They're made out of meat."

"Meat?"

"There's no doubt about it. We picked several from different parts of the planet, took them aboard our recon -vessels, probed them all the way through. They're completely meat."

"That's impossible. What about the radio signals? The messages to the stars?"

"They use radio waves to talk, but the signals don't come from them. The signals come from machines."

"So who made the machines? That's who we want to contact."

"They made the machines. That's what I'm trying to tell you. Meat made the machines."

"That's ridiculous. How can meat make a machine? You're asking me to believe in sentient meat."

"I'm not asking you, I'm telling you. These creatures are the only sentient race in the sector, and they're made of meat."

"Maybe they're like Orfolei. You know, a carbon-based intelligence that goes through a meat stage."

"Nope. They're born meat, and they die meat. We studied them for several of their lifespans, which didn't take too long. Do you have any idea of the lifes-

pan of meat?"

"Spare me. Okay, maybe they're only part meat. You know, like the Weddilei. A meat head with an electron plasma brain inside."

"Nope, we thought of that, since they do have meat heads like the Weddilei. But I told you, we probed them. They're meat all the way through."

"No brain?"

"Oh, there is a brain all right. It's just that the brain is made out of meat."

"So…what does the thinking?"

"You're not understanding, are you? The brain does the thinking. The meat."

"Thinking meat! You're asking me to believe in thinking meat!"

"Yes, thinking meat! Conscious meat! Loving meat. Dreaming meat. The meat is the whole deal! Are you beginning to get the picture, or do I have to start all over?

The response to the story begs the question as posed by the author, "How does a mental reality, a world of consciousness, intentionality, and other mental phenomena, fit into a world consisting entirely of physical particles in fields of force?"

The girl in the woods cries out to me, in my mind's eye, saying, *No matter how much you think you know… you'll never know what it feels like inside me.*

Of course, that is obviously true, for our perceptions

are our own...as far as we know, and yet, when we experience something like the pastor knowing that I was coming to see him hours before *I* knew we must admit that the magic of Life involves much that eludes us.

However, I still don't know what it felt like to be inside her anymore than I believe a learned person can know an *Anxiety Disorder* with panic attacks or *Dissociative Identity Disorder* from the inside out.

Treating mental illness and encouraging mental health and well-being, became the consuming passion of all that I wanted to do for the rest of my life.

At the beginning of the doctoral program, the professors often encouraged us to start thinking about our research question upon which we would build our doctoral research dissertation after all coursework was successfully completed.

The reasoning behind encouraging us to think about the dissertation requirement three years in advance was the unfortunate reality that far too many doctoral students do not know what they wish to research, and as a result, even after finishing all other requirements, they never earn their degree because they can't do a dissertation.

In my case, however, I knew from the moment that I entered the program, the subject of my research. I wanted to know what would happen if the opportunity were ever to present itself again, for a pastor to accompany three well-meaning parishioners to find and help the girl in the woods.

There are many preconceived attitudes people take into such encounters, based on the way they were raised, their belief system, and their expectations. I wanted to research these attitudes to have some idea how people would react, including myself, when given a chance to help someone with mental illness.

Out of the innumerable possibilities and theories concerning the origins of mental illness, I narrowed my research question to a more manageable study of how religious people in a couple of Christian church denominations viewed the source of mental illness.

Did they see possible explanations for mental illness as having been caused by genetics, behavioral, environmental, spiritual, or even Satanic? Isn't it likely that their attitudes would inevitably affect the chosen treatment options?

I have known or heard of many medical providers who, after performing procedures like surgery or medication administration, still believe that prayer or even seeing a priest for an exorcism, is essential to effect a cure.

The title of my dissertation was *Attitudes toward the Etiology of Psychopathology in the Members of a Fundamentalist Christian Church as Compared to those of a Mainline Denominational Christian Church.*

I compared the attitudes of church members from my own denomination, The Assemblies of God, to those of The United Church of Christ and discovered several results that were interesting and even statistically significant. One of those was that Assemblies of God members who would usually believe in the accuracy of the Biblical account of Jesus casting demons out of those with symptoms of mental illness, the *longer* they had been members, the *less* likely they were to believe that demons are the cause of schizophrenia." These results are surprising because my hypothesis was that the *longer* they were members, the *more* likely they were to believe that demons were the cause of schizophrenia. It turned out exactly the opposite.

My suggestions about this surprising result postulated that having lived with experiences of their own in the unexpected changes of life, they arrived at the conclusion that not all illness is the result of sin or Satan, even though such a realization leaves an unresolved conflict in their belief about the inerrancy of the accounts in the Bible. It's fascinating that one can believe something that directly contradicts another belief that is just as firmly held.

Kedric

The realities of life often seem to interfere with the things we have been taught to believe.

Doc

Yeah, like the devastation of finding out Santa Claus wasn't real. Seems like it took months to get over that one.

Kedric

Bringing it up here makes me wonder if you're still grieving. It might be time to get over that.

Doc

Somewhere in there, is a lesson about seeing different viewpoints before making up your mind. A little tough when you're six years old, but a good policy if you ever grow up!

As a Family Therapist with a Ph.D. in Psychology, I would finally be able to develop a treatment plan for the girl in the woods. It would go as follows: Working with the diagnosis that she exhibited florid symptoms of *Schizophrenia, Paranoid Type*, I would refer her to a trusted physician—a psychiatrist if available. After a physical examination and one to determine co-morbidities which could impact her symptoms, he or she would prescribe appropriate medication. When her symptoms became manageable, I would see her in regular psychotherapy sessions. I would probe the peculiarities of her family system, family history, and life events that may have triggered the onset of her condition, while considering that she likely had a genetic component with a predisposition to develop the pathology. Lastly, I would aim to help empower her to be proactive in treating her condition and explore ways she could facilitate her own mental health.

Since she is the primary reason for my further education and training, I am glad to know that, if in the same situation today, I would not simply pray for her, and then leave bewildered. However, if her belief system included the invocation of spiritual blessing or guidance, I would pray for her at the end of every session, as desired, regardless of her religion or denomination, in order to create a trusting atmosphere in which she will be enveloped with the healing power of love.

⚜

Soon after completing my post-doctoral internship in San Diego and becoming licensed as a Family Therapist, I became the Program Director of Yellowstone Boys and Girls Ranch in Billings and moved back to Montana. As part of my salary and responsibilities, a house was provided on campus for me and my wife, Sue, our four children; Clint, Eric, Brian, and Amanda. We ate in the dining room whenever we wanted and it seemed that our lives were finally going to settle down in a place we could stay forever.

However, one of the often-stated consequences of completing a rigorous doctoral program was that it may lead to divorce. Mine was no exception. Having been a full-time pastor with many duties, as well as a full-time doctoral student, meant that something had to be neglected, and it was the marriage that suffered. We engaged in several counseling sessions with the Ranch psychiatrist, but within a few months, it was apparent that the end had come. Leaving my wife and kids living in the house on campus, I moved into an apartment in town.

Staying close to my children became my primary objective, and they stayed with me on weekends, and whenever else possible. Eric, at seven years old, summed up

Moonlight in Mud Puddles

his feelings about the marital breakup and its impact one weekend when he declared, "I like this divorce thing, Dad. I get to spend a lot of time with you, you and mom aren't fighting and yelling all the time, and I get two birthdays and two Christmases with more presents than I ever got when you and mom were together!"

It seemed that everything would work out just fine... at least in the mind of a child.

———

One incident while at Yellowstone is a significant example of my developing style of working with emotionally disturbed kids in crisis. As Program Director, supervising four of the eight lodges on campus, I was often on call to respond to volatile situations when a resident was out of control.

It was a Saturday afternoon when I received a call from the staff at one of the girl's lodges.

"Sarah has trashed her room, barricaded the door, and is sitting on top of the metal wardrobe lockers throwing things when we try to open the door. She also has the music on her boom box up as loud as it will go. If we are going to storm the room to restrain her, we need your permission and presence if at all possible." I told them to wait. I would be there in ten minutes.

When I arrived, instead of approving the restraint procedures, I suggested that I would go in alone to see if I could calm her down. As I pushed open the door far enough to slip in, Sarah threw something which missed but started yelling for me to leave, saying she wouldn't come down without a fight. The

134

boom box was sitting in the middle of the room on the floor with the volume turned up to the max. I reached down and turned it off, and she yelled, "turn that back on, you stupid S.O.B. "

I calmly responded that if she wanted it on, she should climb down and do it herself. She exclaimed, "You're not going to trick me into coming down that easy...I just won't have any music."

I waited in silence for a few minutes and then told her that it would be nice to have music, and suggested we sing together. She looked at me in disgust as I sang "Mary had a little lamb," first in an operatic style and finally with a Blues riff.

Sarah looked at me wide-eyed and loudly declared, "You are crazier than I am!"

At that, we both started to laugh, which broke the tension in the room, and within a few moments, I gently asked what was troubling her so much? She started to cry and said, "I just read a letter from my mom, which said that she was moving away and never wanted to see me again."

I told her that a similar thing had happened to me when I was her age and I knew how much it hurt. I suggested that she come down, which she did willingly, and we sat together on the floor quietly sharing together. I asked if she was hungry and she said she was. When I opened the door, I told the incredulous staff personnel that instead of restraint or punishment, Sarah needed a sandwich.

Years later, I saw Sarah on the street and told her I used that story in teaching graduate students and wondered if she would like me to use her real name. She said she'd be honored to have me do so and added, "My life is so much better now. That was one of the turning points I will remember for the rest of my life!"

———⚜———

After two years it was apparent that my marital situation was not what the Ranch had envisioned, and I began to seek employment elsewhere. I interviewed for jobs in Utah and Texas and upon my return to Billings, found a letter waiting, offering me a position at Horizon Boys Ranch in Goldthwaite, Texas.

In a phone conversation with the Executive Director, he posed the question, "How do you feel about moving to Texas?" I responded that the job sounded exciting, but I wanted to think about it for a few days more.

I suddenly realized that no matter how exciting the job or great the locale, I wanted to be near enough to my kids, to be with them every week if possible. As I pondered my options, I saw an advertisement for a Clinical Director position at Pine Hills School for Boys in Miles City, less than two hours' drive from Billings. I interviewed the next day and was offered the position immediately. The ranch in Texas was encouraging when I told them my reasons, and life was about to provide another new start, which I was certain would be the last I would ever need.

Pine Hills School for Boys is the Juvenile Correctional Facility for the State of Montana, providing different levels of custody and care, depending upon age, court sentence, and risk.

Shortly after my arrival, I visited each Lodge and talked with both staff and boys to get a feel for the place.

Within an hour of my return to my office in the administration building, the chief of security appeared and gravely said, "Well, Doctor, I have a report about you that I have to take to the superintendent immediately."

He went on to describe that one of the toughest kids in the maximum-security lodge had insisted that I was a fake. He said that the school needed to check my credentials immediately because he had been interviewed by at least ten different psychologists and none of them were like me!

I thanked the security chief, encouraged him to notify the superintendent as he saw fit and headed for the locked unit.

The young man sneered at me as he sat down in a room alone with me. He chuckled a little and talked in a tough-guy voice as an obvious attempt at intimidation, "What do you want?"

I looked at him with the saddest expression I could muster, and in a high, whiny voice, said, "I try to be like the other psychologists...I try, and I try, but it just doesn't work!"

I gave him a moment to think about my performance, and then broke into a wide Street-Kid smile and told him I had been a ward of the court and placed in a boys school myself and I didn't give a rip about what others did. I was going to help him my way instead of whatever he was used to. We looked at each other intensely for a moment, before he reached out to shake my hand and said, "That's the straightest thing I've heard in a long time. I'll tell everybody that you're all right, and I'll help with anything you need here."

Having one of the leaders and toughest, yet brightest kids in the locked unit as my "helper" was phenomenal. I was treated with more respect from the kids, even though the staff didn't appreciate my coming right in and showing them up.

I stayed at Pine Hills for two years until my private practice expanded beyond the point I was able to maintain two jobs, and I resigned my position. A few months before I left, the "tough kid," was being released and came into my office, and said, "Having you as my friend here has been one of the best things that ever happened to me. I just want to thank you for not giving up on me in the beginning."

I thanked him as well and told him how much he helped me and thought he would do well in life no matter what he chose to do.

As often happens, I never heard from him again, but remember our time together with much fondness.

I stayed in Miles City for nine years, and my private practice flourished until I had a major blow-out on a road trip to Seattle, and my whole world came crashing down again. I thought that I was finished with my schooling as taught by the "Street Kid," without knowing that the most profound instruction was about to begin, waiting only for the chaos needed to accelerate my education.

11
Mad Indulgence

"I have absolutely no pleasure in the stimulants in which I sometimes so madly indulge. It has not been in the pursuit of pleasure that I have periled life and reputation and reason. It has been the desperate attempt to escape from torturing memories, from a sense of insupportable loneliness and a dread of some strange impending doom."
Edgar Allan Poe

In my wildest dreams, or more aptly, nightmares, I could never imagine becoming a meth addict. No premonition or intuition even hinted at the upcoming disaster.

There was no awareness that I was about to climb to the highest tower on the bridge, and willingly jump off into the deepest part of the abyss. I could not blame any precipitating event or any other person in my life. I alone was responsible for doing the "first line," and of course, I was responsible, many years ago, for doing the last!

The lessons were the most severe that I had ever known, requiring all of my attention, and almost all of my soul.

I did my first line of meth coming back from a road

139

Moonlight in Mud Puddles

trip to have Fish and Chips at Ivar's sidewalk bar down on the waterfront.

Since my time as a Street Kid, I have seen Ivar's as a place of refuge, like Rivendell in *The Hobbit* or Garrison Keillor's *Storm Home* in Lake Wobegon. It's a place where I am well-fed, warm, and safe. A trip to Seattle is always a welcome escape from the pressures of everyday life. Each time I go, I feel renewed by the road trip; the sights, sounds, and smells of downtown Seattle; and Fish and Chips at Ivar's. Feeding the seagulls, who perform aerial maneuvers and various antics to gain a meal, completes the magical experience for me.

The trip itself is a means of self-encouragement to remind me that I have come a long way from my time here, and am able to enjoy the moment without having to wonder where I'll stay tonight or when I'll get to eat at Ivar's again.

I headed back to Montana on Saturday, intending to drive all night because patients were scheduled on Monday morning. I stopped for coffee in Coeur d'Alene and ran into a pool player I knew who said he had a little "crank" to sell me in case I needed it to stay awake on the way home. We went into the bathroom, and I bought a gram in a little plastic bag. He offered a sample line and handed me a short straw. I told him I wanted to wait until I was farther down the road and needed it, so it would last longer.

I didn't want him to know I'd never done it before, or that I wasn't certain I would do it at all. I thanked the guy and hit the road.

Driving in the mountains of Idaho, I became drowsy and was curious to see if it would actually keep me awake, so I decided to try the stuff.

Instantly my nose felt like it was on fire as I snorted a one-inch line through a short straw. My eyes were watering, and I wondered why anyone would hurt themselves so badly, just to stay awake. After a half-hour of agony, I became aware that I felt energetic and was easily wide awake enough to drive all the way home to Miles City, Montana. I felt blurry-eyed and out of sorts for a couple days, and made up my mind that I would never touch that stuff again.

However, a couple of weeks later, I decided to endure the pain, in light of the energy benefit, and I was able to find a little more, to help on an overnight trip to a pool tournament in Missoula. After that, I started to go play pool more often in different places so I could be gone for a few days in order to find and use more crank. I rationalized that I didn't really need it and only used it to stay awake while driving distances like truckers used to do before it became illegal in the U.S. in 1970.

But crank quickly became a form of entertainment, as I chased after the feeling of intense energy and awareness, no matter what I was doing. It truly felt like a positive boost to my sense of wellbeing, and I was oblivious to any negative consequences, because as I said to myself, "What harm could come from simply feeling better?"

Moonlight in Mud Puddles

Kedric

What harm indeed? It isn't as though the pursuit of feeling better drives most of the escape behavior in the entire world!

Doc

Maybe so, but there are a lot of ways to feel better that aren't bad for you.

Kedric

Sure, but trying to rationalize doing meth by invoking that question approaches the height of absurdity.

Doc

Or the height of an enlightening lesson in self-control down the road.

───── ❦ ─────

I was seeing patients in my Miles City office four days a week, allowing three days every weekend for other activities. I had remarried a couple of years earlier, and my wife was supportive of my pool trips, because that had been a good release for me, in times past, and I always came back renewed in mind and body.

However, she certainly didn't know about the weekend meth trips, and I thought I could keep it a secret. I reasoned that all I needed to do was keep it under control with occasional use, and all would be well. It didn't work out quite that way.

The denial was bewildering. Of course, I had to keep

canceling patients and making excuses to my wife and children for sleeping a lot when just back from a trip; and I was beginning to stay away longer and spending more money, but it was still all under control… until suddenly it wasn't.

Without describing any of the highs, or attractions that accelerate the addiction, it's enough to say I was hooked weeks before I admitted it to myself.

In the book, *Expiration Date*, R.E. Wallace, accurately describes meth abuse by saying,

> *"The drug is diabolical in its addiction. It creates a blind spot in the conscious mind that allows the fall to happen without the user noticing the changes, let alone admitting there is a problem."*

I made quickie, drug-fueled friendships, and even though some of them were professionals like myself, we were drawn together by our mutual love of the Monster.

Being up all night with "friends" having nothing in common but chasing the high, leaves few options for engaging in stimulating activities, yet we thought we bonded so intimately, as we listened to music, or just played Yahtzee all night long.

One of my teeth broke in half, and the dentist said I had a really dry mouth. Just one of the consequences of which I was unaware. Within six months the other losses began appearing:

My reserve funds were gone.

My business failed.

My wife and her two children left.

I filed for bankruptcy.

Moonlight in Mud Puddles

It had been just two years since I did the first line and I sunk into a depression and slept most of the time. I didn't do meth much because I had spent most of the funds I had, and it wasn't being given for free... even by my new best friends, who I never saw anyway.

My teenage sons, Clint, Eric, and Brian, lived with me, attending school as usual, except I no longer took them in the morning and I was still in bed when they returned home. I applied for financial assistance and food stamps at the local Social Services office, with a caseworker I had known for years, who seemed sympathetic, while barely disguising her surprise that I was seated across from her filling out the paperwork.

On one of my trips to the grocery store, after presenting my food stamps, the checkout clerk asked me, "Aren't you Dr. Cecil? What are you doing?"

I responded curtly that I was "trying to feed my children." I suddenly had a flash of realization, feeling what it must be like for scores of people that experience it all the time when employees looked down on them with disdain and judgmental disbelief.

Humiliated and exhausted, I rushed home to bury my troubles under the blanket covering my head, and fell back asleep, shutting out the world of pain around me.

After about three months languishing in a depressive stupor, Brian, my twelve-year-old son, woke me up and declared, "Dad, you need to get off your ass, and get on an antidepressant!"

The next day, I called my physician explaining my condition without mentioning the source, and he prescribed a life-saving medication. Within a couple of weeks, I began to engage again in activities with my children.

One evening as we were watching the end of the movie, *Michael* with John Travolta, a Van Morrison song started playing with the lyrics, "Come and go with me, to the Bright Side of the Road."

Suddenly bursting with a renewed energy, I decided that song would be the theme for the rest of my life, and with a regenerated enthusiasm, I stepped back into the light!

I soon found a full-time teaching position at a tribal college on the Fort Belknap Indian Reservation just outside the city of Harlem, Montana, where my mother and step-father as well as my sister and her family lived. I moved in initially with my sister and her husband, determined to do whatever it took to get my life back together. My younger boys, Eric and Brian, moved back with their mother in Billings, but it wasn't long before Clint wanted to start at the college where I taught. We moved together to Havre and commuted the forty miles to Harlem to attend classes.

The next couple of years were filled with excitement and possibilities, and even though I relapsed on meth a couple of times, I admitted it to Clint, and continued to live on the bright side! I was soon engaged in a growing private practice treating patients who also struggled with addictions.

Moonlight in Mud Puddles

I wasn't sure how or why they chose me as a counselor, but I discovered I had an awareness and empathy that could not have been gained any way other than my own journey into darkness.

As with the patients who were surprised by my understanding of anxiety disorders, now I could offer insight into addictions regardless of the substance being abused.

It was so gratifying to offer a new pathway into the light.

I stayed in Havre for twelve years during which I reconciled with my wife, bought a house together, and instead of teaching at Fort Belknap, I became an adjunct professor in the graduate department at Montana State University-Northern in Havre for students seeking their master's degree in counseling. My extensive life experience contributed many rich anecdotes on working with troubled clients, and my full-time private practice offered students internships for those seeking the state counseling license.

⸺⸺

When she retired with twenty-five years as a middle school teacher, my wife joined me in Havre, and shortly afterward, I was diagnosed with a melanoma on my upper right arm.

I had heard the term but had no idea what it meant. Researching it, I found the phrase, "Melanoma is the most feared of all cancers." I read that once the malignancy spreads into the lymph nodes, it could be fatal within months, and further, in most cases it as impossible to know if it had done so until the symptoms became impossible to ignore.

After localized surgery to remove a chunk of my arm around the mole, I asked the surgeon about my chances and how to know if the cancer had spread? He said that with the size and depth of the mole, I had an 83% chance of it not metastasizing, but I wouldn't know until when, for example, "I would be driving along, have a seizure, and they would discover an inoperable brain tumor."

Are you kidding me? The mole that itched and changed shape a little for over a year could kill me?

For the next six months, every time I coughed, my anxiety disorder kicked in, and I waited for the impending seizure to manifest.

My wife and I had been attending a Biker Church with a shelter and food outreach to needy people in the community of Great Falls, Montana, and as I poured myself into the activities, I became less worried about death and more focused on life.

I actually began to view my cancer as a gift, which allowed me to look death in the face, and shout, *Today may be my last, but I'm going to live it to the fullest, no matter what happens!*

A few years later after prostate surgery, my doctor said, "I can guarantee, you will never be bothered by that cancer again," and even though I knew he meant they had caught it early, I felt that way anyway.

Although "Set Free" (Biker Church) was over a hundred miles from our house in Havre, my wife and I attended faithfully a couple of times a week. We decided that since we both liked riding motorcycles and owned a couple of Harleys, we'd get involved in the church's outreach to the motorcycle community and the outlaw biker world as well.

I had heard of the Hell's Angels and also the Bandidos, but didn't know much about bikers at all, other than the movie image of *Easy Rider* with Peter Fonda, Dennis Hopper, and Jack Nicholson.

"Set Free" was based out of Southern California with the motorcycle club named, Servants for Christ. Patterned after outlaw clubs, with by-laws and officers and protocol, I had to prospect for the Servants for over a year before I was awarded the full patch to sew onto a vest, or cut, to be visible over any other garment when riding or attending meetings. I learned that to be in an outlaw club didn't mean a criminal enterprise, but a brotherhood committed to each other, to riding, and to live free from the demands and expectations of society. The serious clubs identified with being one percenters and wore the 1% patch, as part of their colors, identifying their affiliation.

The 1% came from a quote by a representative of the American Motorcycle Association around 1966, saying "99% of the people you meet on a motorcycle are decent, law-abiding citizens." Biker club members, many Vietnam Vets that felt disenfranchised after their return, stood up and said, "and we are the one percenters."

As a Servant, I also became acquainted with members of a Bandido Support Club called the Hermanos. I discovered that the one percent club membership meant a commitment above work or family and recognizing that many are unable to commit to that extreme, support clubs function as part of the outlaw world, yet still keep their normal life as well.

I was a "decent, law-abiding citizen" in Havre, as an adjunct member of the university faculty and a family therapist in private practice—and—I wanted to be an Hermano.

It seemed to me that if I really wanted to be a positive influence in the outlaw biker clubs, I should do it from the inside, rather on the fringes in a church group.

Discussing it with a teacher in a nearby community who was an Hermano himself, resulted in an invitation to be a Probate (or probationary) full-patch member, and soon after a club vote, I became "Hermano Doc" in the largest Bandido Support Club in the world, with a brotherhood reaching as far as Australia.

I neglected to discuss it with my wife, however since she was visiting family out of town, but I was confident she would support the idea. I also waited to tell the pastor of Set Free in Great Falls, believing that he would enjoy having a new connection to the Bandido Nation through a member in his own congregation.

I was wrong on both counts.

The pastor was quite displeased, resulting in my hasty departure from further attendance, and my wife was upset with both of my decisions in her absence.

The "Street Kid" seized the opportunity to run away in a new attempt at freedom, and while my wife and I decided to stay together, I started going on long weekend trips to hang out with my new brothers.

I should have known that running away always led to chaos, but I ignored the signs because I was truly convinced that I was "On a Mission from God" as quoted by Elwood in the *Blues Brothers* movie.

It was to be a meaning-filled mission all right, but one directed by the president of Street Kid University!

My intention in joining the Hermanos was to bring a sense of spirituality into the brotherhood. Many, if not most of the outlaw clubs, had a state chaplain to be available in times of need, for counseling, weddings, and funerals, but that sounded way too much like being a pastor, and I wasn't looking for another failure.

Besides, the Montana club already had a chaplain who had been a full patch holder for many years and doing a great job. He was a man who had proven himself to be a solid club member and brother, that could be depended upon, and was the epitome of the club maxim, "Love, Loyalty, and Respect."

When we first talked, I told him that I really wasn't looking for any position in the club because I was hoping just to learn to be a good brother, like himself, and that was enough for me. He had known me previously as being with Set Free, and also that I had been a pastor, was a therapist, and a university professor, and "spoke for the whole club" in welcoming me as someone who would have a great impact as an Hermano.

I immediately started to ride to club activities and events to meet brothers in chapters in Helena, Great Falls, Kalispell, Billings, and Missoula, making an initial impression that I fit in well. We soon started a chapter in Havre with the school teacher that had sponsored me, and three others: a wheat farmer, a musician, and an oilman. We started our own weekly chapter meetings, always inviting motorcyclists from around the area, in hopes of expanding our chapter to include anybody who thought it was cool to be an outlaw biker.

I didn't tell the others, but in addition to the sense of belonging, I thought it was really cool to dress up in my biker outfit. The entire Bandido Nation (the one-per-centers and many support clubs) all wore the colors of red and gold. When I dressed up, it was with red and gold shirts, bandanas, pins, name tags, and the crowning glory of my cut with the three-piece patch that depicted Hermanos at the top, a sombrero intertwined with a motorcycle fork in the middle and "Havre" on the bottom. Every time I wore the outfit, I felt like I had as a cub-scout, and even though I was in my fifties, I became like a kid again. It was fun.

Unfortunately, I soon discovered that most of my brothers identified with being *real* bikers, and certainly not like cub scouts, and I still felt that I was just pretending.

After two years, I was no longer a Probate and earned my diamond with the number 13 in the middle, designating that I was a full patch holder in good standing.

Soon after, at an event, the State President put forth my name as the sergeant-at-arms, responsible for keeping order among the troops and providing discipline when needed.

Moonlight in Mud Puddles

Within months, the State President was elected as National President and asked me to be the National Sergeant-at-Arms of the Hermanos Motorcycle Club!

I was in the second highest ranking position in the nation, respected among *real* bikers, including the one percenters, but I still felt like a poseur that liked to play dress-up.

It wasn't long before my standing in the club started to unravel. I had relapsed a couple of times on Meth, intending to show that I was really hard-core, but instead, I experienced a paranoia because I had so much to lose if I became addicted again.

The National President was completely against illegal drug use when representing the club, and feeling his disapproval, I resigned my position. Several months later, on a club trip into North Dakota, the new State President slugged me on the shoulder and told me to "shape up."

It has always been a policy of mine that a friend need only hit me once to cause a serious impairment in the relationship. Regardless of the intention, when he hit me, instead of embracing the admonition to "shape up" I decided to "ship out" and rode back to Montana alone, knowing that it would be seen as resigning from the club.

Within a few days, the State President called me and said I would not be considered as being out bad, meaning that club members didn't have to shun me as excommunicated, but I was out of the club, primarily, as he said, because "You are not a biker...I don't know what you are... but not a biker."

He may not have known, but I did... I was a pretender, as I had been as a "Street Kid" and perpetual misfit, that was really going to miss fitting out in my Cub Scout outfit.

———————

I still refer to myself as a "Meth Addict," not because it holds any attraction for me at all, but because I have learned the potential devastation from sniffing one small line, designed to keep me awake on the road home to Montana.

I have once again been able to use the immeasurable lessons to offer help to meth addicts, bikers, and even pastors who all just need someone who really understands.

I also still identify myself as a "Misfit" and yet in spite of every misguided moment, if that allows me to show others their own way home…it will have been worth it all.

12
A Time To Heal

"Health and well-being can be achieved only by remaining centered in spirit, guarding against the squandering of energy... maintaining harmonious balance of Yin and Yang... and nourishing one's self preventively."
Nei Jing
Yellow Emperor's Book of Medicine

Breaking the cycle of addiction requires a major change in the way we think about everything. Addictions manifest in different forms but have one overriding trait in common. They are dominated by a misguided attempt at self-soothing to the exclusion of everything and everyone else in the addict's world.

Sometimes, no matter what becomes our motivation or how badly we truly want to quit, change is only possible because of a significant wake-up call.

My daughter, Amanda, had just given birth to twin boys a few months earlier. Having recently retired with an impending divorce, I moved in with them until I found a place of my own. Uncertain about my future and feeling displaced and discouraged, I decided to go shoot pool in

155

Moonlight in Mud Puddles

a local hangout.

When I went into the bathroom, I ran into a guy I knew, about to snort a line of meth. Turning to greet me, he asked if I wanted "a little bump?"

It had been several years since I used any, yet for reasons beyond my comprehension, I bent down and sucked it up into my nose.

Immediately I left the place and jumped into my car with my mind screaming, " What did I just Do?!!"

I felt desperate because I knew I couldn't hide it from my daughter and her fiancé, who had his own history with it. I didn't really want to disguise it anyway.

When I got back to the house, I told them both what happened, and went down to my basement room feeling like each step descended further into a bottomless pit.

After a little while, Amanda came down and sat in the recliner next to mine. She told me that she knew I felt bad and that she loved me as a dad and grandpa, but wanted to be certain I understood they couldn't have it around the boys.

I suddenly realized that regardless of any future impulsive moments, my grandchildren were worth far more than any temporary gratification, and it must never happen again.

I responded to my beautiful daughter with an absolute resolve that, not only did I understand completely, but also reassured her the twins were enough motivation to abstain for the rest of my life.

There were other motivations as well.

I wear a bracelet on my right arm, which never comes

off. It was given to me by my granddaughter Natalie, who was only nine years old at the time. We were having lunch together for what we both knew would be our last time since her grandmother and I would soon be divorced, and her mom wouldn't let her see me anymore.

We reminisced about our time together over the years, and even though we were not biologically linked, we always bonded as though we were.

Suddenly, Natalie took off a stretchy child's bracelet which was bright green with metallic silver spots, and as she handed it to me she exclaimed, "Hey Ric…maybe this could be our thing!"

Surprised and astounded that a nine-year-old would even think in such terms, I readily agreed and told her that I would get it placed inside a clear tubing of some sort, wear it for the rest of my life, and leave instructions to take it with me into eternity.

I had already stopped using meth a few months earlier because of Silas and Atlas, but "our thing" is a constant reminder that my grandchildren are as precious as life itself.

My newest granddaughter, Torrin Skye, born two years ago, continues the motivation…as do my own children, Clint, Eric, Brian, and Amanda, who have been my inspiration, even through all the troubled years.

And finally, myself, for while my kids and grandkids are like the air of life, believing in myself, is the breath of love that brings it all together.

There is no doubt that one of the consequences of my descent into the world of addiction was the impact it had on my children. My relationship with them, their respect for me, their viewpoint of who I was and what I had become all suffered as a result.

Conversely, the benefits of my chosen abstinence impacted them in much the same way, because the pathway of healing will have a positive influence for generations to come. Being constantly aware of the presence of my children and grandchildren in every impulsive moment, became a way of thinking that transcends far beyond breaking the addictive cycle.

Kedric
It's awesome to have children and grandchildren as a motivation not to mess up, but that doesn't work for everybody.

Doc
That's true, but everybody has something that they want more than the momentary high and the subsequent plunge into oblivion. They just have to search for it and make it happen!

As I forged ahead in new ways to actualize self-empowerment, I developed **Seven Principles of Personal Transformation:**

I. Wish Not, Want Not:
My mother often used the adage, "If wishes were

horses, then beggars would ride."

This was usually a criticism of some childhood disappointment such as, *I wish Humpty Dumpty had been more careful,* or a host of other childish regrets. When I heard this edict as a child, I had no idea how powerful and providential it was to become as I engaged in the change process.

I was parked along the country road near my mother's house where my wife and I last lived before the divorce. The house sat on a little hill with a big fenced yard, surrounded by inspiring cottonwoods which reached almost to the river's edge. It was a beautiful place where I had walked with my dog, thinking, *this is where I want to live for the rest of my life.*

This time, parked along the road, thinking about what might have been, I started to say to myself, *I wish…*when suddenly the voice inside my head interrupted and proclaimed *Wish all you want, but you can't have it both ways. Like everything else, what happened here is either a tremendous life lesson or a tragedy you must regret for the rest of your life. What's it going to be?*

Instantly I knew that I must reframe my thought processes so that instead of ever allowing myself to wish …I must interrupt my rumination…and thank my teacher for another life-changing lesson.

II. Thought Challenge:

Our thought life consists of everything we hope for, and everything we will ever be.

Throughout my life, aberrational thinking has propelled me from one crisis to another. Guilt, anger, condemnation of self and others, alienation and insecurity, have all fueled my misguided attempts to escape to a magical place where I can fly, eat whatever I want, and be a kid forever, without responsibility or accountability.

As I began to think about the impact a potential action may have upon my grandchildren, I realized I possessed the power to say "No" to myself, and imagine the outcome with a totally different perspective. I then progressed to an application of the principle into every thought which embodied negative potential. Even in absent-minded thought, I practiced catching myself in mid-sentence and challenged it. *I've had two types of cancer and I bet more is… "Wait! That's not how I feel…I appreciate life so much more now.*

Moonlight in Mud Puddles illuminates the thought challenge to be either "mired in the mud or be moved by the moonlight." It takes practice to catch yourself in the middle of every negative thought or action, but because practice makes perfect…perfection is the direction of your new life's journey.

III. Celebrate It:

The application of "Wish Not, Want Not" and "Thought Challenge" principles brings the realization that every experience of life is worthy of celebration. Not because of any moment that was painful or tragic, but because of the amazing lessons and opportunities for personal growth. The storms of life are often viewed as calamities to forget and put behind us, but attempting to ignore significant events is an exercise in futility. By celebrating them, we remove their power to bring pain with every remembrance, replacing instead, immediate awareness of the power positivity creates in every moment. Celebrate even the deepest sorrow, for it's in the darkest places that we awaken to the brightest light.

———❦———

There is a mysterious, spiritual connection which exists between trauma and awakening.

A former patient who was blinded by an accidental gunshot at the age of sixteen exemplifies this amazing correlation. When Fritz first came for therapy he had been without sight for over twenty years. As we discussed his initial feeling of discouragement, it soon became evident that he had a gift of sight which far exceeded anything normal vision could reveal. Fritz frequently displayed a sensitivity to the unspoken needs of those who were privileged to be his friends. He often seemed not only to know of some hidden hurt but also have just the right words or insight to bring a healing balm.

Fritz often asked what I was looking at, as I turned my attention toward something. When I asked how he knew that I was diverted elsewhere, he replied, "I saw you look." He invited me to know how he "saw," by instructing me to close my eyes and visualize a TV show with some movement or action being portrayed. I knew Fritz liked *Bonanza* as one of the shows he saw before his accident. I told him that in my mind's eye, I could see the Cartwright family on horseback in the shows opening sequence. He said, "Can you see Ben's big smile or the difference in size between Hoss and Little Joe?"

As Fritz took me on a visual tour of the scene in my head, he exclaimed, "That's how I see everything."

While I began to understand "how" he saw, I still was baffled by his vision of the unknown and the feelings of others in his world, who were often separated by physical distance. But he just seemed to see and know.

In an attempt to relate to the unknowable, we experienced several therapy sessions in which I was blindfolded.

As soon as I entered his home, I experienced an awareness of fear, followed immediately by a total dependency upon Fritz as my teacher and guide. I was forced to relinquish any semblance of control, and in doing so, felt a bond of trust which strengthened, as my teacher led me to *see* something new by touch, or sound, or deeper awareness.

In the movie, *Oh Brother, Where Art Thou*, following an encounter with a blind prophet, the following exchange occurs between two of the principal characters:

> **Delmar:** *How did he know about the treasure?*
> **Everett:** *The blind are known for their sensitivities compensating for their lack of sight, including psychic powers.*

My nickname for Fritz was "The Prophet," and the goal of therapy was simply to help him become more aware of his wonderful gifts, his value to others who needed his wisdom and insight, and to help him learn to celebrate, rather than condemn, the tragedy that birthed them into existence.

Of course, the awakening of inner sight is not limited to the blind, nor does the trauma need to be physical. Dr. Bessel van der Kolk states,

> *"I have met countless patients who told me that they 'are' Bipolar or Borderline or that they 'have' PTSD, as if they have been sentenced to remain in an underground dungeon for the rest of their lives, like* The Count of Monte Cristo. *However, none of these diagnoses takes into account the unusual talents that many of our patients develop or the creative energies they have mustered to survive."*

For all whose experience has unlocked new potential, the realization that the pain gave rise to healing is certainly a cause to celebrate it!

IV. Boundaries:

In the past, if I had any concept of having a boundary, it meant to control the behavior of others who got too close, like a line in the sand over which they were not allowed to cross. But what happens after the line in the sand is drawn if the other doesn't respect it and crosses anyway? Unfortunately, the answer often is, that we simply move the line because we love them, or don't want them to be unhappy or don't want them to have another meltdown which may reflect badly upon us.

Many relationships are devastated because parents, spouses, lovers, or friends, are without boundaries and allow others to run over them with impunity. It often

Moonlight in Mud Puddles

begins in childhood as well-meaning parents attempt to set limits upon strong-willed children, who have learned that "No" only means they have to try harder because the parent has no clue how to back it up.

Picture a mother in the candy aisle of a grocery store with a precocious five-year-old, who spots a favorite candy bar, before the frazzled mother can sprint past.

"Candy...Candy", the child states, urgently, yet still calmly. Mother responds, "No, it will ruin your appetite, and you won't eat dinner."

Even more urgently, and much louder, the child insists, "Candy, I want candy!"

This exchange may go through a few more attempts, as both accelerate the intensity of their positions, but as they begin to yell at each other, shoppers start to take notice. The mother interprets their disdainful looks as saying, "What is wrong with that mother? I wonder if that poor child is being abused at home. Maybe we should report this to the police."

Burdened by a screaming child, and her mistaken interpretations, in which her child may be taken away... she finally gives in, telling the child, "Okay, you can have one...and you can hold it until after dinner and eat it for dessert if you eat all your peas."

The child smiles quietly and agrees, but as soon as her back is turned the child rips off the wrapper and takes a bite. The mother turns around just in time to see her sweet-five-year old throw the rest on the floor!

The mother quickly leaves her groceries, picks up her disobedient child, and hurries out of the store, with fleeting thoughts of homicide—or suicide. Instead, feeling guilty, she decides to keep him from being further upset because he's crying that he wants more candy. *But, he's usually so nice…I better put his favorite TV show on to help him calm down, while I prepare leftovers for dinner. All I really need is just a little peace and quiet.*

The reality of this scenario (and many others regardless of age or relationship) is that until we learn to say "no" and make it stick… we can never truly say "yes" because giving in is really just giving up, and the other person has manipulated us into uneasy compliance.

Proper boundaries are essential to having healthy relationships and are predicated upon the conviction that my limits exist for my protection and to serve my purposes, but not to control others.

In the groundbreaking book, *Boundaries*, by Cloud and Townsend, the statement illustrates clearly,

> *"You cannot change others. More people suffer from trying to change others than from any other sickness, and it is impossible. What you can do is influence others. But there is a trick. Since you cannot get them to change, you must change yourself so that their destructive patterns no longer work on you. Change your way of dealing with them; they may be motivated to change if their old ways no longer work."*

"But if I tell him no…he will think I don't really love him," a father says of his adult son, "and wind up going downhill, or worse."

However, the truth is that real love may require the

Moonlight in Mud Puddles

parent to let the adult child go, allowing him to become independent, make good choices or not, and learn the way everyone does, giving a chance for both to live full and productive lives.

Good boundaries are essential for personal growth because they teach us when to say "no" and when to say "yes" for the ultimate benefit of all concerned.

V. Having Enough:

It's wonderful to live where we are free to have "Life, Liberty, and the Pursuit of Happiness." But when your pursuit is driven by a lust for money, power, or fame, neither happiness or liberty will result as you become a slave to the acquisition of *more*. We live in a society that embraces spirituality and success together as being evidenced by God's blessings to give the faithful more. More food; more of everything; more than we could possibly spend or use in many lifetimes, supposedly because we are loved beyond measure, above all the poor and destitute peoples of the earth.

The truth is just the opposite.

No spiritual teacher or wise sage in history has ever taught that having more than one can use, and living extravagantly, is the pathway to health or happiness or spirituality in any form.

The western culture that identifies itself as Christian and often embodies the ideal of a Prosperity Gospel seems to have little in common with *Jesus*, as presented in the New Testament. Even though he is often presented as having the power to have anything he wanted, for some unknown reason, he chose to live without houses or lands, rejected expensive clothing or furnishings, and frequently distanced himself from the "religious rich" of his day. It would certainly seem that he knew the truth of God's blessing but obviously didn't equate them with having more.

Lao-Tzu, born over 2500 years ago, and recognized as the author of a little volume of poems and verses called the *Tao Te Ching*, lived his life in relative obscurity. The *Tao Te Ching*, which has been translated all over the world, contained wisdom that would surely have allowed *Lao-Tzu* to be a renowned and successful teacher in his own time, had he chosen to release it and develop a following of disciples. Instead, he was the keeper of the emperor's library for at least fifty years, and only released the scrolls of wisdom at the end of his life.

Mohammed was orphaned at the age of six and was raised by extended family members. It is reported that even after becoming a man of means, he always lived simply, was humble, friendly and kind, with an emphasis upon caring for orphans and the poor in a poverty-free community.

The Buddha was born into wealth and luxury, yet chose at the age of twenty-nine to become an ascetic, wandering in poverty and seeking freedom from the attachments of the world.

The list can go on indefinitely: *Gandhi, Mother Teresa, the Dalai Lama,* and a host of teachers, philosophers, and leaders throughout the centuries.

How do you know when you have enough? When

your focus in life is to be a blessing to everything in all creation and *looking beyond your own needs*, you discover the true meaning of Life, Liberty, and the Pursuit of Happiness.

VI. Giving:

Once we realize that we have enough, a transformation occurs that releases us from greed, the acquisition of things, and the fervent seeking of wealth, status, or power.

We become far more able to embrace the journey inward to find our true selves and the purpose and meaning that brings life into all the world.

Learning to establish boundaries (so that we are not ravished by vultures) and realizing that we have enough to meet our basic needs (without having to pursue that which will never satisfy) we become free to seek opportunities to give our time, talents, and money to those less fortunate, whether rich or poor.

I love to shock rich people by giving items of value, because everyone assumes they have everything anyway. Thus they are often void of the surprise gifts that are so reminiscent of childhood. Their reaction is priceless as they exclaim, suspiciously, "You're giving this to us?"

I usually get the same response from homeless and impoverished people when I can give a fifty-dollar bill,. They look at me wide-eyed, wondering what I really want. It's so much fun to see their faces when they realize there are no strings attached.

With the mindset of giving, it is a pleasure to negotiate more than the asking price or tip a server twice what they might expect. It is such a privilege to also give my time and anything out of my available resources. Each day I open myself to giving, and sometimes it's almost miraculous how those in need seem to come out of the woodwork.

How can I give so much, and so often?

The simple answer is that I am richer than anything money could ever provide, and I fulfill my deepest calling when I can be a blessing to others in both the animal and plant kingdoms, wherever I go.

VII. Into the Flow:

When I visualize the flow which brings synchronicity and harmony into everything, I often think of the animated movie, *Finding Nemo* as the Australian current whisks all sea creatures along at a pace much easier and faster than any could produce by individual effort alone. In my mind's eye, I see the current flowing just above my head, and if I quit struggling to make it happen, and release myself into it, all the **transformative principles** come together as one, and I am carried into the blessings of love, in which all life is renewed forever.

There are two large seas in the Middle East bordering Israel, Syria, and Jordan in the present political and geographical borders. They both have the same source of water, which originates in part from an underground river emerging into a beautiful garden at a place called

Moonlight in Mud Puddles

Caesarea Philippi in northern Israel. The water flows into the first sea, which is clear and deep, and, is teeming with life, both in and around its shores. It is called "The Sea of Galilee."

The same life-giving water forms the Jordan River. Flowing quickly and freely, it brings vibrancy to everything and is known as the "River of Life" in many ancient writings and stories.

With its journey complete, the Jordan River brings the same clear water to another sea. No life is present in its depths, or around its shores for miles. There are no fish, no plants, no community of people or children playing on its banks. Nothing! It is called the "Dead Sea."

But why doesn't the River of Life, bringing the same refreshing water, produce life in the "Dead Sea" as it does from the moment it creates the beautiful flower and plant garden at its source?

The answer is a simple and yet profound metaphor for the meaning of everything we love.

Every drop of water that enters the Sea of Galilee, it *gives out*, and every drop that enters the other, it *keeps*, because the Dead Sea resides at one of the lowest places on earth, with no outlet available to let the water be renewed! As a result, the water stagnates, evaporates in the heat, and allows no life to exist.

We always have the same choice: seek to gain as much as possible; or release everything we have and everything we are into the flow.

It's a choice between life or death!

The Seven Principles of Personal Transformation are not an attempt to suggest deceptively simple solutions to complicated problems. However, simplicity often provides insight which is most profound, if for no other reason than it is easier to remember and actually works.

The wake-up-calls, and the lessons, both tragic and triumphant, propel me toward an awareness of what's really important, as I choose to embrace life in all its glory!

13
Connected

"Intuition is really a sudden immersion of the soul into the universal current of life where the histories of all people are connected, and we are able to know everything, because it all written there."
Paulo Coelho
The Alchemist

Life is such an incredible journey. When we learn from yesterday and live in the present, we are liberated in the future.

Those who have been traumatized as children are often stuck in a past that is too painful to remember, yet too poignant to forget. The past often feels too frightening to face, the present ready to erupt into chaos, with a future that promises only more of the same.

But, when we celebrate the experiences that have taught us so much, a transformation process begins that will revolutionize our entire lives.

We have to look at our teachers and the lessons they have provided: From the **Street Kid** I developed a belief that I can survive and even thrive, regardless of my circumstances.

From the *Therapist*, I found that hurting people needed someone who was educated, experienced, and professional, but even more someone who had worked through their own issues enough to facilitate the healing process in others.

From the *Misfit*, I learned that conformity to the expectations of others does not necessarily produce contentment, and I can appreciate my own, and others, uniqueness.

From the *Approval Junkie*, I discovered that a positive self-image does not come from seeking the opinion of others, but from changing the way I feel about myself.

From the *Pastor,* I understood that attempting to meet the expectations of everyone is an exercise in futility, yet each person deserves as much attention as possible.

From the *Meth Addict,* I was astonished to find how rapidly an insidious addiction could dominate my life, and in addition to relating to the feelings of a welfare recipient, it became clear how vital self-discipline is in maintaining health and well-being.

From the *Professor,* I realized that the experiences I often viewed as only a failure, gave insight and perspective to help students achieve success.

From the *Parent,* came the greatest lesson of all, as I recognized that the best gift I could give my children was to get myself back on track, and to keep trying, no matter how many times it took to make it happen.

Of course, I have also graduated from the schools of

the P*iano Salesman, the Naval Deckhand, the Bartender, the Fast Food Server, the Child Care Worker, the Lineman, the Shoe Salesman,* etc., to name a few.

It is so gratifying to know there are times we can make a positive impact upon the lives of others, not only in spite of our issues but, in fact, because of them.

The key to opening the door to this possibility is to understand that *everything* which has transpired to this present moment, offers the potential to enhance our own and others' lives if we pay attention to the opportunities as presented.

———

When I think of the life lessons which have shown a pathway out of pain and devastation, there is none more powerful than an experience written by my mother in her book, *Journeys of the Heart.*

She writes of a time when I was fifteen years old, a ward of the court of the State of Oregon, and placed by a juvenile court judge in the Vancouver Boys Academy.

After moving with my little sister out of the house of her abusive second husband, she was trying to do everything she could to provide a loving environment as a newly single mother caught in the throes of marital, family, and financial crisis.

This is a story of the real survivor in my own life's journey as she fought to bring the power of love and light into one of her darkest places.

"You can't come in yet, Mother," nine-year-old Libby called *through the locked front door. "I'll be ready in a minute."* I

Moonlight in Mud Puddles

could hear our little chihuahua barking and some movement in the house. I had just returned from work in downtown Seattle and stood waiting, somewhat impatiently, my arms loaded with school books, until she finally let me inside.

Then I saw the table covered with a lace cloth. On it were two lighted candles. "I made dinner for us, Mother. For a surprise for you." I took off my coat, laid down my load of books and quieted Candy, our noisy little dog. Then I was seated at the head of the table set for two, and Libby brought in a bowl and placed it in front of me.

"I only could make a can of hash, Mother. I didn't know how to make anything else. But we like hash, don't we?" I assured her it was one of my favorite dishes. We bowed our heads and gave thanks to God for his goodness to us-and I fervently thanked God for my wonderful little girl.

We ate the hash and catsup by candlelight, and it tasted like ambrosia! We weren't being nourished by hash alone, though. We were being strengthened by love and courage and determination.

We had been deeply wounded, and joy seemed to have disappeared when Libby's father left us for a new life. All the members of the family were confused and devastated. Her older sister married young and left home. Her teenage brother was in a boys' school where he could find guidance and healing. Only a few months before, we had been a family of five around our table, but now there were just the two of us.

We tried to keep a family spirit and started several new customs, such as decorating our home every month for the holiday season. If there were no special day that month, we thought of something we could celebrate with small decorations and cheer.

176

It took effort, imagination, and courage to try from day to day to rebuild a home out of the hurt, but we kept on trying. Libby was showing that same spirit when she served us hash by candlelight. Although only two of us, instead of five, sat at that festive table, love was there. As time went on, we realized that the God of love was with us all that difficult and lonely time, guiding and gently healing the raw hurts. Now, I have been re-married for many years. My oldest daughter, Kathie, has a good life with her husband, two daughters and seven grandchildren. My son is a counselor who ministers to the wounds of others, understanding them better through his past hurts and broken dreams. Libby grew up into a fine woman at whose table I have had many excellent meals.

But in my heart, the best meal of all was the one she pre-pared for me the night we had hash and courage and love by candlelight!

Relating to "Hash by Candlelight" brings to memory a magical demonstration of the power of love that I saw, a few years ago on the streets of Portland, Oregon.

One of my true joys, when I am in a big city, is to go downtown where the street people hang out to see if I can connect with someone and maybe help a little.

I met "Breezy" with her boyfriend and hung out for several hours doing things homeless people couldn't usually do, as I had a rental car and a little money. Of course, Breezy wanted to drive, and despite being unsure if the insurance still covered it, I gave her the keys. The excitement on her face made it all worthwhile as she drove all

Moonlight in Mud Puddles

over Portland. Her boyfriend (whom I won't name, out of respect) and I, had similar backgrounds, and he knew a mutual friend from the past, which further enhanced our sense of trust.

Describing Breezy is as difficult as trying to understand the immediate bond between us. She was in her late twenties, bright-eyed, tiny, and a ball of energy, with a quick wit and sharp mind.

I connected with her boyfriend well enough, but with Breezy, I felt that I was meeting a family member that I knew and loved from another place and time.

I soon had to fly back to Montana, and after exchanging phone numbers, I dropped them both off downtown.

A few months later, I called and asked if I could interview her about life on the streets, and after setting a day and time to meet, I drove to Portland with a couple of friends.

I talked with a couple of documentary filmmakers about doing *A Day in the Life of a Girl on the Streets* and followed Breezy and her boyfriend around for a couple of days to get a feel for it.

At the end of the second day, she suggested that we all go eat downtown at her favorite Chinese restaurant. Even though I had just given her a hundred-dollar bill for the interview, and paid everyone's expenses, I thought it would be an excellent ending to a great time together, no matter what it cost.

As we neared the restaurant, Breezy spotted a homeless girl she knew, and said, "Hey, we're getting Chinese Food…come join us," which she gladly did.

Connected

The six of us, Breezy and her boyfriend, the street girl, my two friends, and I sat at a round table and were served delicious Chinese food, family style.

After a couple of hours, laughing and just enjoying the moment together, I reached for the bill, but Breezy was too quick. "No way, Doc," she said with a big smile, "This one's on me!" She produced the hundred, handed it to the server, and said, "keep the change."

Walking out, I felt like part of the entourage for a beloved movie star who blessed everyone just by her presence.

Breezy was far more than that to me...she was one of my heroes...displaying the true meaning of love as an Angel of Light!

A few months later, I received a message that she was gone after an apparent overdose.

I was shocked and saddened, yet, I celebrate our time together, and as I try to follow her example, I am honored to have been one of many whose lives she chose to touch.

My experience with Breezy initiated the beginning of a deeper awareness of the meaning of life and the interconnectivity of everything that brings it into existence. As I reflected on who she was, and why she chose to be homeless on the streets, I began to see things in a different light. She was bright and capable and could have easily found a profession in which her intelligence and exuberance would enable her to be successful, and I

179

wondered why she hadn't chosen that route. Of course, logic would suggest that she had a drug problem which kept her down, but I have known many professionals who were addicted, and still maintained the appearance of success, at least on the surface.

It began to dawn on me that perhaps she did have a profession, in which she was highly successful. She was a Street Angel who brought energy and encouragement into a world which desperately needed her gifts.

Is that possible? I wondered. *Could it be that gifted people are stationed at every level of society to bring new life, and instead of being lost, they are offering a service which could not be found any other way?*

For many years, I realized that failure often breeds success, but I thought it was simply a triumph over tragedy, without viewing both as essential to the process.

Does the light need the dark in order to shine? Does health need illness in order to manifest true wellness? Does life need death in order to regenerate? Do street people need others like Breezy in order to flourish?

As a society we often view people who are homeless or standing with a sign on the corner as not being willing to work or put forth effort to change their situation, but perhaps they do not determine success by the standards of society. Perhaps their goal is not to meet the expectations of others, but to bloom where they are planted, at least as long as they are rooted there.

I had a recent encounter when I saw a girl on a corner

with a sign asking for money. A thought flashed through my mind, "She could at least lay a story on me, face to face, like I tried to do as a runaway on the streets. As I stopped at the red light, I thought her face looked familiar, and I asked if I knew her. She exclaimed, "Dr. Cecil, do you remember me? You were my therapist in Havre (250 miles away) ten years ago!"

I pulled over and chatted for a while, gave her all the money in my pocket, offered some words of encouragement and hugged her goodbye. She excitedly said, "I'm engaged to be married and am doing so much better now. I can't wait to tell my fiancé I saw you!"

As I drove away, I was struck by how much the encounter meant to me.

Note to self: *Everybody's on their own journey and no matter what, I must never be judgmental about anything people do to survive!*

I am reminded of the wisdom in Hermann Hesse's book, *Siddhartha:*

> "In every truth, the opposite is equally true. The world itself, being in and around us, is never one-sided. Never is a man wholly a saint or a sinner. This is a stone, and within a certain length of time it will perhaps be soil, and from the soil, it will become plant, animal, or man. I do not respect and love it because it was one thing and will become something else, but because it has already long been everything and always is everything. I love it just because it is a stone."

Moonlight in Mud Puddles

I have fallen in love with life!

I now see the entire earth as alive and find myself loving everything. I love the rocks and the mountains, the birds and the insects, the air and the wind.

I have fallen in love with the process that allows life to be regenerated and renewed, and the incredible cycle of life, as evidence of a love that is eternal.

As Neil deGrasse Tyson relates, we should

> "...embrace our genetic kinship with all life on Earth and value our chemical kinship with any yet-to-be-discovered life in the Universe, as well as our atomic kinship with the Universe itself... We do not simply live in this Universe. The Universe lives within us."

One of the most profound examples of love in the physical world is the process of photosynthesis. As the energy of sunlight with the green plants of the earth, it is converted into sugar and oxygen. It produces and maintains the oxygen content of the earth's atmosphere and supplies all of the organic compounds and most of the energy required for all life on Earth.

It is a beautiful example of love because it does not exist to sustain its own life but to sustain all life.

Photosynthesis requires both light and dark cycles in order to function as one reaction is light dependent, and the other reaction is light independent.

As humans, we often see the light as good and the dark as evil and want life to exist without sickness or death.

182

But in what Lao Tzu calls "Earth's mysterious generative force," we witness an amazing cycle in which all forms and manifestations of life are regenerated forever.

Call it by any scientific label you like. To me, it is the most obvious attestation to the existence of love created by intelligent design. Everything is interconnected and part of a truth that is way beyond our comprehension.

The noted Neurosurgeon, Dr. Eben Alexander, states,

"We see the universe as a place full of separate objects (tables and chairs, people and planets) that occasionally interact with each other, but that nonetheless remain essentially separate. On the subatomic level, however, this universe of separate objects turns out to be a complete illusion. In the realm of the super-super-small, every object in the physical universe is intimately connected with every other object. In fact, there are really no "objects" in the world at all, only vibrations of energy, and relationships."

Each molecule is in harmony and balance. Each plant receives and responds within the flow. Each person is so connected to everything that when we respond in appreciation, all life reaps the benefits.

Call it synergy; call it spontaneous combustion; call it symbiosis—it seems like love to me.

We often view love as being a human emotion, but when all the forces in the Universe conspire to bring an incredible balance and harmony into everything imaginable, love is literally "in the air" in an exquisite dance with all creation!

Moonlight in Mud Puddles

———— ✦✦✦✦ ————

I have experienced what I refer to as a quarter turn in my thinking. I do not reject any of my beliefs, or that of others, even though many are utterly antithetical to each other. They are all part of the whole, which in itself, is bigger than we could ever imagine.

I still believe in God. How could I not? But now I see God as way beyond my capacity to define or understand, except as declared unequivocally in countless writings and experience throughout history: God is love.

Further, I believe love is the greatest force in the entire Universe, and brings everything into an incomprehensible balance and harmony, producing life for all eternity.

Albert Einstein is quoted as saying,

> *"Everyone who is seriously involved in the pursuit of science becomes convinced that a spirit is manifest in the laws of the Universe. A spirit vastly superior to that of man, and one in the face of which we, with our modest powers, must feel humble."*

And as Neil deGrasse Tyson says,

> *"The scientific study of the Cosmos is spiritual—even redemptive—but not religious."*

Every moment of my life, sick or well, anxious or calm, tired or energetic, I celebrate the closest connection I have ever known with God. Love is everywhere (omnipresent). Love is all-knowing (omniscient). Love is all-powerful (omnipotent).

I have an awe-inspiring appreciation for things that I

would have paid no attention to in the past, but now it feels like we are all energized by love, and the best way to make an impact is to let it flow.

I am, of course, still a street kid and a therapist, who is working on my stuff, and a pool player who often pretends to be a hustler, and a misfit who is often misinterpreted by some social blunder, and an insecure loner who overcompensates with a confident bravado...but other than that, I've got it pretty much together.

And I love, *Moonlight in Mud Puddles*...because sometimes, when I feel stuck in "it" up to my ears... The Moonlight is the only thing that reflects enough inspiration to pull me through to the other side!

You owe it to yourself to see it.

Life is incredible!

The Conversation Continues

Doc

So now we need to talk.

Kedric

Bring it on, Teacher Man.

Doc

At the end of *Wisdom from the Streets*, we talked about telling the whole story, but it seems a lot has been left out.

Kedric

What? We wrote about the change that turned us around in the first place…and the drug scene…and more lessons from failure than we could ever have imagined.

Doc

But, what about Pastor Perry knowing we were coming fours hours in advance and how and why Challenge House? What happened to all that, and how did it even occur in the first place?

Moonlight in Mud Puddles

Kedric

If I knew *how* it happened, my brain would probably explode, but, your right. I did leave out a few details, like getting the money together and the plane ticket to New York.

Doc

And what about the FOG... and a host of things that seem nothing short of miraculous?

Kedric

I've had a lot of that during my entire life, but still don't have an explanation, even when it happens to others in different religions and all walks of life.

Doc

Also the Dark/Light continuum, which seems important. Even if you don't know how to explain it, you should still tell the whole story.

Kedric

Wow, that's a whole book in itself!

Doc

Exactly. I think that you...I mean WE...should write one more book about Spirituality and the Miraculous and even include the stuff that really isn't either one, but is still pretty cool.

Kedric

Well, it would be good to tell the whole story.

Doc

Only don't wait so long to get it out this time.

Kedric

Okay, you win. You remember it happened one time when I was on the run, and...

www.ingramcontent.com/pod-product-compliance
Lightning Source LLC
LaVergne TN
LVHW051629080426
835511LV00016B/2256